Spiritual Beings:
Being Human

Annette Moss
with Mark Firth

Copyright

Spiritual Beings: Being Human

Volume 1

First published by Love and Light Books

(www.annettesloveandlight.co.uk)

© Annette Moss 2017

British Library Cataloguing-in-Publication Data

A catalogue entry for this book is available from the British Library.

ISBN-13:978-1979842877   ISBN-10:1979842876

Printed and bound in the UK by CreateSpace.com

Dedication

For seekers of knowledge from here and beyond –

And who for those who have walked alongside us,
helping, guiding and guarding us -

With love and light from

Annette

Acknowledgements

I would like to personally thank my soul-mate, Phillip: You inspire me every day even when I don't always find the words to say. My world became brighter when you walked into it. Also I'd like to thank Phil for designing the covers for all of the books in this series.

Thank you to Mark Firth for the many conversations and your contributions which have led to writing of this first volume, and for our friendship.

Thanks also to:

- the Ascended Master Djwhal Khul for his channellings and patience;

- Archangel Michael for his omnipresence and protection, and for allowing me to paint him and use his picture for the book covers;

- St Peter for his protection and wisdom;

- my family on the earth and in spirit for their love and guidance throughout the years;

- Angela's patience when scribing my words – your assistance in this book, and the others in the series, is invaluable.

Contents

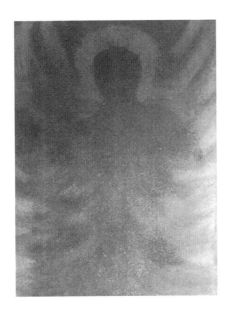

What makes life Extraordinary...

Appreciate the ordinary

Introduction

Why did we feel the need to write this book?

We feel that the common denominator for a spiritual being is how difficult it can be, and to also remain human, when all you may want to be is a free spirit.

This book in particular is an overview of the physical world from our spiritual perspective.

It was developed from two human beings having a conversation – and a number of similar conversations which have taken place over the last five years.

At times the conversations have gone in different directions due to the nature of the discussions and to put things into context in book format, spiritual beings have come forward to assist us – so this book has been written from spirit to spirit for spirit.

In a sense, this book represents our spiritual writings.

What we say should not be taken as "rules" for living, these are our suggestions of how you could do something, how you might feel, what you perhaps could say.

In life, there are no "should"s – it is a word that is commonly used to control someone.

We prefer that you "could" choose to do something.

This first book lays the foundations for other books to follow.

Each chapter contains some blank space for you to record your thoughts on any questions posed within it, or which arise from your reading.

You may also want to write some journal notes – but if you prefer to write in depth, there is a series of accompanying journals which you can use.

"Life is the tapestry of being a human being and the threads that bind it together": Annette Moss

Spiritual Beings:

Being Human

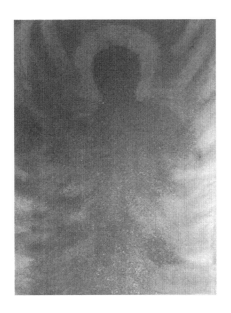

The best relationship is one that comes from within.

Trust in yourself for you are powerful — and the best friend that you can give to yourself.

1.   Personal responsibility / Being Authentic

Personal responsibility is a choice we all make to accept our decisions and choices. We constantly make judgements in our lives and right or wrong is an example of this inner judgement. What may be right for you may not be right for someone else – and if it feels right to you, should you follow through with it.

A judgemental attitude is based on the conditioning formed from a belief system whether it is ours or someone else's. Our action may cause harm to others because we have judged ourselves to be right.

The plan
Is there a grand plan to life, a spiritual plan?

The question of 'is there a plan to life?' as opposed to living our lives without responsibility was posed and we considered the duality of life and our how are decisions may affect others around us.

How we choose to live on this planet could have a positive or negative effect on others, is it for their benefit or will it cause them harm, if it does cause harm are we then responsible for their pain. It is also a personal responsibility how we decide to respond to others pain. This is our personal responsibility.

How can you make an informed decision about something when the information given to you could be from somebody else's perspective or agenda?

Is right or wrong a perception that we have learned from others, our family or peers?

At what point do we sit back and question the bigger picture – how will my actions affect others, and then decide what path to take in the future?

As a spiritual being, it might not bode well within you– if you are told to go and commit some act? An act that may go against your inner gut feeling, we are not talking about committing an atrocity – we simply mean from a general perspective. Does our response come from a place of fear? Is our decision coming from fear – because if it is, we need to take a step back.

Inaction can also arise from fear. This inability to make a decision is fear based.

Sometimes is it easy to go with the flow of life than go against the current of life and leave decisions to others.

For example wanting to leave a toxic relationship could be put off because to actually do it would mean leaving your home, and cause emotional and financial disruption.

This 'putting off' itself could be perceived as fear based. We may need to remove ourselves from that fear before we take a more conscious action and proceed?

Actions

Every action causes a reaction, one of the basic premises of karma.

In order not to react out of unconscious conditioning, we instead create an "anti-action" – for example, breaking the mould of behaviour, an abused child growing up and actively deciding NOT to become an abuser themselves shows powerful personal responsibility. It is about the sudden wake-up call, the midnight epiphany, and the profound moment of deciding "no more!"

Challenges

Throughout our lives we are met with certain challenges.

If we don't master the challenge it may return to us at other time in the future. It may not present itself in the same way but the outcome may be the same. How we respond to the situation is down to ourselves.

Being authentic within our lives when dealing with other people is paramount and helps to release the emotions rather than storing them for another day. E.g. By putting the lid on an emotion, such as anger which can often be shut away then may manifest as repressed anger which manifests in other areas of your life. Resentment is another form of anger directed at someone.

Resentment can fester and grow eventually become poisonous to the person feeling theses emotions but it can also affect others. We may have to cultivate a responsibility to ourselves so that we can deal with our own personal feelings. Communicating our feelings will help and promote harmony with ourselves and others around us. If we are a more balanced person with our feelings our stress levels will be reduced and we can deal with situations better.

Please use this space to record your responses to any questions which are either posed in this chapter or which arise from it.

Questions:

How did this chapter make you feel?

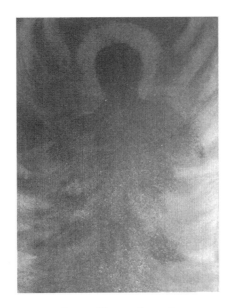

Guardian Angel...

If I was an Angel what would you see...

*All beautiful and bright, with a
shimmering light...*

With a halo of love for you, from me...

Forever protective all golden and white...

If I was an Angel, this is what I'd be...

Guarding you always, blessed be to thee.

2. Health and Wellbeing

Sometimes it is easier to focus on another's pain because it detracts from our own. Our emotions can be seen as our inner ocean, if it is wild and stormy we cannot see what is underneath, or see what is causing our emotional distress. You may then discover your own shipwreck within the ocean, the remains of what caused the emotions but are yet to discover what treasures are within it. The treasures of our inner self: if you do discover them would you acknowledge and value them? If you are helping a friend by all means engage and help them with their situation, but be aware of avoiding your own situations.

A mind that is in the dark, un-acknowledging the cause of emotion, can allow fear to grow within. You could be experiencing an overwhelming sense of sadness about a situation. If you delve into sadness you may encounter the unknown which automatically stirs fear. The unknown can bring great trepidation but to face fear can bring about new insights, calm the mind and promote change within and without.

Facing fear with love, love for yourself and for others is key and moving from love to unconditional love could take a lifetime to understand, for loving unconditionally goes beyond the human love conditioning.

The question often given to myself as a therapist is "how can I move forward in my life without my ex in it?" Learning to be self and one to one with your own being can help to propel you forward into your own self-love relationship.

Being quiet in the peacefulness of your own mind is a difficult exercise for some. As is quietening the mind of continuous thought.

Why do we become so hung up on relationships? Is it because we are used to being a collective/ where to some being part of a relationship is paramount whereby to others it is inconsequential. We come into this existence alone and at the point of exit alone but yearn relationship during physical life.

Is it a yearning to be accepted that propels us into a relationship? Your divine chi is out of balance and this is why there is a desire for acceptance from another: whether it be a parent, sibling, partner or someone in authority.

The mind can have its own agenda. By reprogramming the thought process, it will have a new direction. One that is fuelled by a new sense of wellbeing for self.

On a spiritual note, we as human individuals recognise that for growth we need teaching.

Being a physical being and being able to express yourself with your partner.

How or how much does the body react to energy?

The energy of the body works from when you're born – you're born to a particular family.

In order for the soul to grow to its highest potential – the birthplace, subsequent astrological configurations, the age of the parents, other family members and the conditions of the environment, are all taken into consideration.

Before we are born, we choose the life that we wish to live. During our life there are many lessons that we want to learn. We choose the parents and the DNA from which our body will be made up. It's quite a complex mechanism creating a body.

Pause for thought – what if, after all the choosing that we go through, the process of choice that we make when choosing our body and the learning process that we want to have during that life, what if during or after the foetal stage something in the make-up of the body goes wrong? This can mean that the body suffers illnesses that we didn't choose, didn't "sign up for" in the choosing process.

Is it, then, a consideration of the location of where we are actually born – can that have a part to play, that if we have free will our parents may choose to use certain drugs whilst we are in the womb, or they may choose to be with a partner who has a sexual disease – these choices can inflict on us?

Also, doctors can make mistakes during the birthing process which leave the baby starved of oxygen – there are many factors in our lives that we cannot choose about. We cannot blame everything on spirit – but what we can do is make the best of the hand that we have been dealt.

There are so many inspirational people on this planet who, through adversity, can stand tall – even if they have no legs.

Is it at that point, then, that your higher self comes forward to help you find the strength to make it through your trials and tribulations?

Another thought – the curveball – what if you didn't choose this particular path, but a higher being chose it for you, to help you with your soul's purpose? Being human, that's when we turn to thinking "why me?", when it really may have been chosen for us, for a higher purpose – to either help you or others in some way.

If we then think about children and school and learning to have a balanced diet within schooling, that's conditioning – informed by the parents and environment and friends. It is what children are introduced to.

All food has an energy.

Having fresh food on a daily basis has a higher energy. Its lifeforce gives you a better balance rather than processed fast food.

Scientists know that anything cooked starts to lose its life force – so by the time something goes through its ready meal process possibly zero energy nutrients are left.

Your body makeup experiences different foods in different ways – some people might be more tolerant to certain processes.

There's a school of thought that your body type makeup will sustain itself from different foods in different ways.

If we look back to olden times, giving thanks for the food – you were putting energy into that food by blessing it and thanking for it – that's the act of gratitude, which is spiritual in itself, you're not just grateful for food, you're grateful for life.

The blessing method is that you accept that whatever you want in your life is already there.

The same goes for fluids, we can ask for healing energy to go into water and then drink it with the intention that it will purify your inner being.

Our bodies are 85% water so if that life-force goes in and you imagine it spreads, it will go round the body and push out the impurities that we hold onto. This is the excretion process, through urination and defecation. This is our body's way of expelling the rubbish that it no longer needs.

So when we put food into our body, let's look at why we do it? We need it to fuel ourselves. But are we wanting food for fulfilment or do we just want to feel full? Finding out which, helps us to maintain a healthy vehicle.

If you listen to your body as to what it wants to fuel it – and you feel that your body is saying it wants chocolate, do you then feed it chocolate? Why is it craving certain things? What is it in chocolate that you are craving, for instance? Look at your food groups and your fluid intake? What is it about each item that you like? How does it make you feel when you are eating or drinking it? Do you like the taste of chocolate or the feel of it melting in your mouth? Do you like the crunch of a chip or the taste of it having been fried? When it comes to fizzy carbonated drinks – is it the bubbles and the fizzing sensation that you like, over and above the flavour? Equally, what don't you like about some foods or drinks? How do you like your egg? Some like scrambled or fried but hate poached. There are so many ways to cook an egg – what is your preference?

By looking at the food and fluids that you ingest you can get a better picture of who and what you are like. And if you feel you are craving something more, you can find a lower calorie version that will fulfil you – life is not an all you can eat buffet!

There may well be a medical reason why you feel a craving for something – pregnant women experience pica, the medical term for craving different or sometimes strange items to eat or drink. Some women report having licked coal during pregnancy, whilst others craved meat even though they were vegetarian.

Whilst growing up we can choose not to follow the family food traditions, and choose consciously to be vegetarian or vegan.

Some children will no doubt not be given that choice, growing up in a vegetarian household – and then make a choice later.

How does their body then process / break down the food then if they suddenly start eating meat which they have never eaten before?

If you live a more organic life your body will start feeling better.

When you digest unprocessed food you know it has little chemical enhancement and mentally you feel better, more healthy – so you're eating energy improves – it's like a psychological placebo effect. You believe you will be healthy – so you are. You condition your mind to feel more well. This then takes us to stress and how stress can have an impact on certain people.

The effects of stress

Stress releases chemicals in the body which may affect us – toxins. The body's pharmaceutical production plant is out of whack with the world around us. We reach for a chocolate bar because we want a quick fix of sugar or DMT (a chemical) which is a stimulant which will make us happy for a few minutes, then we will go back down to our unbalanced state from that rush.

There are lots of different diets around but the best form for the body is your mind as your mind can dictate what you want to put in it and what it feels like.

Sometimes a little bit of what you feel like having does you good, as it might give a quick sugar rush but give you enough to keep you on the go again.

It's the comfort eating that's a problem – at that point, why do we need to do that? Why does your body and your mind tell you that you need to comfort eat?

Because of the chemicals – but also because that stressful part that's in you needs that. We lead more stressful lives now, so we require more quick fixes. We feel out of balance in our lives.

Stress and anxiety affect the body in different ways, both mentally and physically. If not addressed, it could cause you to have changes within your body and lead to a series of medical conditions.

How can stress affect the body? The more common side effects are: lack of sleep or too much sleep, headaches, problems with the bowels and indigestion. it can also affect the nervous system. should you find yourself in a stressful situation or have been in one over a period of time, seek the help of a GP or qualified homeopath, a trusted friend, or a qualified psychotherapist, to talk about your feelings. Sharing the problem, such as the old adage of "a problem shared is a problem halved". Either way, you are important.

Irritable bowel syndrome is a medical condition that can affect your inner health and your whole being. the symptoms are stomach cramps, lethargy, loose stools and constipation. it can also affect your body temperature - perhaps it is your body's way of alerting you to certain situations. are you feeling you cannot let go to certain situations? are you holding on to fear, thus your body is resisting release? But by holding on to waste can harm the body, keeping toxins within it. So some questions to consider then are: am I holding myself back and why? If so, what am I holding onto? Why am I allowing myself to be ill, or why am I making myself ill? What energy do I not want to step into, or is it that I am comfortable in an energy and resisting its change in stepping beyond my comfort zone?

We are not, of course, saying that you necessarily have Irritable Bowel Syndrome because of who and what you are - it could be due to a number of issues, like diverticulitis, Crohn's disease, having a sensitive bowel or parasites etc, as there are other factors to consider here.

Similarly, stress can have an effect on other illnesses such as Fibromyalgia. There are lots of self-help groups for this condition, and there seems to be an increased trend in the diagnosis of Fibromyalgia. The problem is not that you are being lazy - you may feel shattered and exhausted, because you do not have the energy to do something. Hidden illnesses such as this can be very difficult to cope with - illnesses which cannot be seen by other people. For example a broken arm or leg can raise sympathy or empathy from others - but not an internalised illness. Or a mental health condition

How can you determine, or should you determine who is valid as being worthy of such as status. This may also cause some people to think of benefit fraud etc. The lack of understanding from others can make the effect of the illness more painful for the sufferer as they feel misunderstood or unacknowledged.

It is becoming more acknowledged now that there are many hidden illnesses - but for many there are no known "cures" - they can be maintained or managed, but not cured.

In our society, when we greet someone with "hello, how are you?" not many people respond positively when the person they greet says "I'm not great, thanks, I'm having a really rough time of things at the moment". How many people today would actually stop to have a conversation with you to listen if you were to respond like that? Some people don't have the time, the energy, the inclination, the desire to listen. But as a spiritual being, if you were to take time to listen to someone about their problem, could you be taking the problem off them, giving them healing, or just giving them the acknowledgement of their illness and their importance to you.

What does it say of the person who doesn't listen? Might it be that they don't have the ability right now to give time? It may not be their fault that they are not able to be open to you right now - so don't let the exposure of your vulnerability allow you to feel rejected by someone who isn't able to offer you their time or attention.

How do you avoid this trap? Just say "hello" to someone, and then decide what you add to that - "how are you?" if you have the time to offer to them, or "lovely to see you, but I have to dash" if you don't. But don't ask how they are, if you are not prepared to listen.

We have a huge interdependence as human beings - we are always dependent on others. This comes to the forefront, for example, when we split up with a partner and the ownership of the joint goods, chattel, children, pets etc is decided - do we split up from their family and our joint friends? Who gets custody of our social life when we used to get on so well with the in-laws or the friendship group which we shared with our partner? Bringing a new partner into the equation then brings in even more issues.

Breaking away from the cycle

As we know, the fear of the unknown stops us from all achieving our aspirations on many levels.

The thought process is that throughout our lives if we change how we perceive things, this may help our inner being to come out to help us to go forwards in our life and not be scared, not have that pressure which is outside source and also we put ourselves under pressure to go forwards as well.

Is it unrealistic or realistic? That's something to think about? Can we do something about, and if we can, why aren't I? Do I really want to do it? I say I do, but if I'm not doing it, why aren't I?

For example 'I would really like to go swimming and I enjoy swimming but what stops me is walking out in my bathing costume. The question is why?

Does it matter what someone else interprets your body as? The body is a beautiful thing – a mechanism.

It all goes back to fear which brings on the stress once again.

At what point does the body really speak its mind, and do we ever listen to what the body tells us?

This all comes back to fear – the greatest fear of all. It is a big topic!

A visualisation exercise

Step into the fear - what are you really afraid of? This is a creative visualisation exercise: please find a comfortable position to begin this exercise.

- Visualise yourself in a bright white light, and imagine that you are feeling carefree. Imagine a box beside you, with the word "Love" written all over it, on the top, bottom and sides. Place whatever it is that you are afraid of in the box, together with all the negative words connected and associated with this fear.

- Then write all the positive words - I can do it, I am amazing, I am capable, I am love and I am loved, I am beautiful, I am fit and healthy, I am free, I have boundless energy, I have clarity of mind, I have a healthy bank balance - these are examples of a few words that you could use to empower yourself. Place these into the box. Close the lid and shake the box up.

- The positive phrases will overpower the negatives in the box, and disempower their meanings.

- Now, imagine that you open the box and allow all the positive words to flow out, and see them gently float out of the box and into the sky. When the last one comes out of the box, close the lid and then put a lock on the lid. There is no key to open this box again. Now, looking at the box, visualise it getting smaller and smaller and smaller, and so small that you can hardly see it, it's like a speck of dust. And just like a spark of light, it disappears.

Joining energies

At the point of entry, two energies join together and this will depict what vibration these two energies are at this time. Within a relationship one may grow and develop and surpass the other. The one left behind may feel lost and may not realise what has happened and look for an alternative partner.

The one developing will then look back and feel betrayal, but this is where the unconditional love, thoughts and feelings are learned, knowing we never lose anything – just that there is a beginning, middle and end to a relationship. This can be obtained in many areas of your life: you enter university, at degree level you develop to attain your PhD through researching what you have learned in the past. This is called the University of Life.

Exercise

How to be yourself with the eyes of another?

Ask a friend or partner to realistically view you as a human and as a spiritual being.

Please use this space to record your responses to any questions which are either posed in this chapter or which arise from it.

Questions:

How did this chapter make you feel?

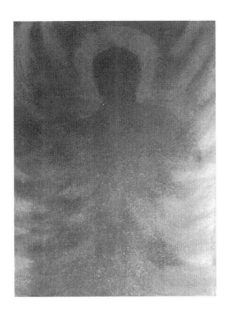

*To wear your armour is to know you in
battle -*

Step back and release your freedom.

3.   Being a spiritual bitch

Being a spiritual bitch doesn't mean you have to be nasty or retaliate. It is not a boxing match.

There can only be one winner in that match. This is not a competition.

This is about standing in your personal power and not allowing someone to have glory in defeating you.

There are many rounds in a relationship.

All relationships have a natural ending, remaining true to yourself throughout the relationship and through turbulent times shows strength of character.

What does 'spiritual bitch' mean? Being true to yourself is the most important part of our human existence – therefore some people would say that if you are not wanting to do something for somebody else, they might say you are being a spiritual bitch.

But it's knowing when to say yes and no – being authentic to the spiritual, not the human. It's only someone's judgement, the ego's interpretation of a bitch – everyone's is different.

Going back to being authentic spiritually, that's where it's most important.

Maslow's triangle of needs – physiological, safety, love/belonging, esteem and self-actualisation.

You do have to stand in your own personal power, being true to yourself.

"I don't want to go to work today because I want to be at home. But I want to go out and do something" – that's an inner strength.

From experience of being in relationship where you are not being your true self, you're not being true because you are maybe not aware, or perhaps you are acting for somebody else, fitting yourself into a certain kind of role.

But if you put yourself in that role, why did you? And what was it about that role that you felt you should engage?

Let's say you are a person who is charming a potential partner and you realise that you are unable to sustain the glamour, when you don't have the finances. The potential partner may feel that they are not worth the expenditure – When embarking on a new relationship, perhaps be open from the beginning and share the experience in the romancing of each other.

So being a spiritual bitch may be a bit of a misleading title – it pertains to men as well as a women.

Should we, be a spiritual bitch? If it means being authentic and true to yourself, then yes! As long, as it's not hurting anyone else, resulting in causing offence. Being authentic can be subjective and down to the interpretation of others. It is a bigger subject than the spiritual bitch aspect.

It can also be standing up for yourself in the workplace – by saying something is not acceptable, being assertive, taking control. This is what others are maybe doing in the workplace – people can be stuck in repeating situations.

For example: when people are perceived to being unkind, you may recognise this, and wonder what to do about it – you may need to be assertive, stand up for yourself and deal with the situation.

When a person realises that they are aspiring to learn within all their areas of life, by being able to stand within their own power and uses the voice in expressing when something is not acceptable. This is a spiritual lesson that could unfold for an individual.

Throughout our lives we relate differently with different people and at times need to reaffirm our independence. Remembering to empower our human being. This will feed into the relationships and friendships chapter.

Please use this space to record your responses to any questions which are either posed in this chapter or which arise from it.

Questions:

How did this chapter make you feel?

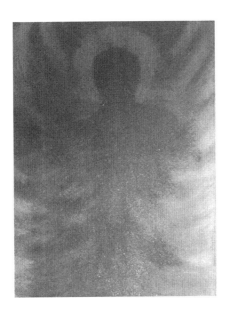

Meditate and allow the elders to channel the healing elixir through the vibrations.

4.   Relationships and friendships

We said earlier, when you are born, you are born into a particular family.

We were talking about energy, where you are born etc. and the relationship which you can have with your mother or father – if one is missing, who takes over the parental role.

Do you have a parental guardian or is it another guardian, are you a guardian of state?

Who do you look at for your role model and how does that shape the rest of your life from birth?

It does shape you – early informative experiences, we know from psychological perspective. From a spiritual side, we know that the soul has chosen the relationships.

We might not be aware of that – we all have fallout in our relationships, even if relationships with parents are good there are always areas we can learn from.

This gives credence to a life of learning – you might think, how my parent was with me, I will never be like that with my child or in my life. How can I be different from my mean father? I will be generous.

That can be dangerous in some respects as you are trying to be the opposite to what your role model has been.

Let's look at why was father mean with money… Was it that he didn't have any as a child, and his safety net was to hang onto it? As a human we might think he's not generous, not forthcoming, but it will have been his conditioning, his thought process. As a spiritual being we need to look at all sides.

It's a domino effect – what his father had, and his father and his father. It's ancestral impact and ancestral conditioning which can affect the now.

How ancestry can impact your now – that would depend on where you were born geographically.

From a spiritual aspect, they have looked deep into the ancestral line of your family, even though you might have no ancestral connection with them – you are placed where you need to be.

The ancestral programming forms the lifepath in adolescence.

Then, depending on the relationships you have had with your peers growing up, that can have impact on your adult relationships – what do you want in a friend? Look at the friends you have, are they similar to yourself?

To continue the move forward – when we leave this body and another soul is placed in my grandchild to carry on its blessings. It's very abstract to try to think of this. Like ley lines – it's a spider-gram of your ancestry.

We say we don't choose our family – but spiritually we do.

We DO choose our friends.

Colleagues at work are of great importance to us as we learn a lot from them – they might challenge us workwise but also in personal life.

As a spiritual being, working in an environment of people who are not spiritually thinking, it's very challenging as they are more grounded in money and financial terms, whilst we aren't.

Going into the relationships that we choose – if you are not conscious when you engage in a new relationship, then you might follow the patterns you followed in the past and experience the same issues that you have followed previously.

Only when engaging consciously we can see patterns, that the person is triggering something in you, pushing your buttons – only then can you choose to take a new direction, continue the relationship and modify your own behaviour, or change / depart from the relationship.

Within our life we may need different energies to be within our lives, so we may choose certain friends because of their energy and their thought processes suit what we need – we might not have very much in common, but they bring something that you need to have as nourishment for your soul.

We have to be very careful – if you are a spiritual seeker, you may only try to make relationships with other spiritual people and not take anyone else into your life, not engaging with the human as much as you want to work and live with just the spiritual.

Being spiritual and living amongst those who aren't conscious, who are asleep, blissfully unaware of what a spiritual person has to go through day in day out.

It's all conditioning within our society: what we are, what we think we are meant to do. Meant to have a job, a house, responsibilities.

Then at one point the spiritual person realises this does not fit with me, it's not what or who I am. Is that then labelling us and putting us in to a glass jar with a lid on it?

You will be in a job, with family, 2.4 children, house, family car to suit everyone's needs – you will do for everyone else.

That's not being who you are if you are a spiritual being – we don't want to have a deadline, have constraints of time. Time is irrelevant. Be who you want to be. Feel well as you are – but as a human you have to do those things. That's the work relationship.

If someone as a spiritual person feels that conflict inside, it's how to maintain a balance – maintain a job and look after themselves. It's a balance. It makes you question what you choose for your life, we choose how we want to live.

To go for a job interview – seeking particular job roles, you have to attain particular educational standards to do that job – we know the path of what we need to do. As a spiritual being you don't know the path. My thinking on this is – whatever you put your mind to will come about.

If a 17 year old wants to become a lawyer they will put themselves through the right education to do this. They might then suddenly get a spiritual awareness which tells them, no, they don't want this.

How do they move on from that and balance life and work with existence?

Looking back again to olden days where men were main breadwinners and women stayed home to look after the family – whilst some women would have liked to have gone to university and studied but the family role was to be home with children.

When children grew up, then the woman starts thinking "what have I done with my life?"

Apart from the children, then you can look at the job roles – home, mother, wife, cleaner, nurse, lover, confidante, counsellor, teacher, gardener, etc. every job is done within the household, book keeper, organiser – a multi-tasker.

You've done everything, covered a multitude of things without being paid for it.

So then what does this woman do when she has an empty nest – she has all these skills, but no single specialist subject matter to go into the workforce.

So she panics – what can I do for me? I'm coming up to half a century, what do I do now?

Then deal with menopause, knowing you are not going to have any more children, the body saying "no more now", a big dilemma.

A life dilemma – what's the relationship in the rest of life. An existential dilemma. I've been THIS – now what?

The issue could also be the relationship with the husband at this point. Did we have one in the first place, when did we lose it, when did it change?

A fundamental wakeup call to say "what have I done with my life? And from now onwards"?

You may then be a carer for your parents – having parented your children, questioning your own existence, your relationship with your partner, asking how you can reclaim that or make a new relationship, possible retraining for a job that you might have wanted to do in your teens – and then your parents are elderly and need looking after – so the dilemma comes in again – do you give up yourself in order to look after them?

Then there's the relationship with the older generation and how do you manage that?

So then – are you going to be a spiritual bitch and look after yourself? Are you going to have an awakening now and have time for yourself?

Now you can recognise that you have time to develop that side of you!

Going back centuries – women will have had this dilemma throughout. It may be slightly different from now – but still a big change.

How to keep your mind active when your body is slowing down and not being as active as it was when you were looking after the children – now that they have left, you don't maybe need a job as you're financially secure.

You might not be outgoing, not have friends, you are on your own 8 to 10 hours a day waiting for husband to come home.

Husband comes home tired, wife is looking for emotional contact and not getting it. Relationship is suffering because he doesn't want to talk / have sex with her – he may be questioning his own life.

He may be questioning why she doesn't dress up for him anymore? She's been home all day - the lifestyle choices that we make have an impact in the rest of our life.

The relationship with spouse – being taken for granted – keeping it a relationship of love through all this change – that takes a lot of work. In that instance, if the wife stops taking care of her aesthetic self, who is the relationship with – are you taking yourself for granted?

Letting yourself go – or taking it for granted that your looks will always be there. Your weight might change. Life changes – essentially you are not looking after you.

That's when the need to be a spiritual bitch comes back – if you haven't got a relationship with yourself, how can you have one with anyone else?

Some people – men and woman – like to potter around the home, have people round, be in the garden – happy with their bubble. How big is your bubble and when do you burst it to go into the next? Then are you forever blowing bubbles?

Moving forward in a new relationship, trust is the main theme – trusting yourself within a new relationship. How can you trust yourself not to bring a past relationship into the present, because things will come up. A relationship in the now always brings other relationships up, whether positive or negative.

If it's negative, you need to think – don't repeat patterns, or don't get into the same trouble.

We're talking about a relationship do-over within the new.

Previously we talked about cutting ties to past sexual partners – but also we need to cut the ties to past relationships, so that no energy from these are taken forwards. Reprogramming ourselves, to allow someone new in, to view them with fresh eyes – and learning the lessons of the past – "I needed to go through that to go forward now".

It all comes back to trusting yourself and having crystal vision when you are multi-faceted person, knowing that whoever you meet along your travels will also be a faceted being.

Juggling relationships

It's hard when we have several friends who are close to us – how much of their time we seek, how closely we hold them to us, what their friendships mean to us. If our friends fall out, how does that affect us?

Let's say, for example, that one of our family members has an argument with a second family member, and this fractures the family unit. Two of the most stressful times with regards to relationships are weddings and funerals – who to invite, who to leave out, who will feel offended, who sit with whom, who gets invited to the evening party or the church event, who gets to have an input in organising, etc? And let's not forget Christmas – which set of parents are we going to, or inviting to ours, for Christmas dinner?

We might want to invite everybody to an event, but we know that grudges between people may fracture their relationships, making it hard to involve both parties.

Who is controlling what and whom here?

There will always be a choice. You can choose whether you want to be involved in deciding who to invite or not, or whether you choose not to let a fractured relationship hold any power over you.

At the end of the day, please remember, you do not hold the glue and it is not responsibility to "fix" the fracture by yourself – but you do have a responsibility to yourself to be happy. And if it means saying "no" to the people who are causing a difficulty, then maybe at the wedding it may end up just being you and the groom, or maybe at Christmas dinner it will just be you and your partner – or at the Christmas party with a smaller number of people. You are not responsible for other people's thoughts – you must have your own.

When attending events, somebody could well be upset about those attending – whether it is a wedding, funeral or a party of some sort. You are not going to please everyone.

Wedding situation: table planning. Sometimes you can arrange your tables as to think who you think would sit wherever – but why not let people decide where to sit? Please spare a thought for the bride and groom who may spend hours sifting through the invitations in the hope of getting it right.

Funeral arrangements: there is a small amount of time within the funeral service to be able to read a eulogy. There may be special moments that you might feel have been left out, but these are YOUR special moments and thoughts, and the person who has passed away will know that they are your moments and will remember them with you as part of your relationship. Do not take offence if your particular moments are not mentioned, or there isn't time within the funeral service to include as many tributes as you would perhaps like.

Your children's birthday parties can be another bugbear – you might have given your child ten places to invite friends in the preceding weeks, but what if your child then falls out with somebody in the meantime and makes two new friends? Will you allow extras to attend?

Part of being human is having and making allowances for change because life is subject to change.

Another aspect in relationships is that of being taking for granted or giving too much of yourself, or feeling out of control in a situation.

An example of this could be sharing your lunch with a colleague at work – or a child doing so at school – and then feeling aggrieved when they do not share back with you on another occasion. But do we share for the purpose of having someone share back to us? Do we not share for the sheer point of sharing and giving?

We might go out of our way each morning to give a colleague a lift to work because they claim to have sore feet, but whilst at work they stand and walk around for eight hours. Where is the control here? The colleague who is taking you for a ride by asking for a lift to work? You for giving them a lift? Who is taking who for a ride?

You might buy someone a bunch of flowers because you want to do it for them – but they question why you have bought them, saying "I don't like flowers". Where is the control here, and how do you feel at their response? Do you then not buy that person anything again in the future, or do you put this one incident behind you and move on?

At all times, we are the person who is control of how we feel about a situation – nobody can make you "feel" anything – we choose how we feel or respond.

When relationships end

When replacing one person with another in our lives, what does this say about us and the need to be fulfilled in a relationship?

Is it the illusion of need?

If a partner dies or leaves, and we find another partner immediately, or two weeks, two years later, when is the right time?

Spiritually we are all one – it's the human that instigates a timescale. We are self-limiting, we tell ourselves we will recover in a certain way or in a certain time.

How much control do you have? Can we dare to be our ultimate controllers?

We can control when we die – to an extent. We can control our destiny, our fate. We have been taught so much that we cannot control certain things, but others prove that we can. We all have our own self-limiting beliefs.

If you believe it, it will be so. This goes on to our Soul Purpose.

We limit ourselves in so many ways. Ask yourself:

Do you believe in me as a writer and as a medium? Do you believe in our editor's ability to edit and create? Do we believe in you? Do you believe in you?

In writing this book, one of us has doubts about what will happen with it, whilst one is confident that it will be very successful. We both know however that we have to write this book – and the successive ones afterwards. It is important for us to write and finish and publish this book – it is the domino that starts the chain.

Friendships

Being authentic within a friendship can help to bring balance. A give and take friendship is always the healthiest. Perhaps when you find that you are always the giver, this could bring a divide between the friends, if not acknowledged at least by one of them.

There is no ownership in friendship – it's a two, three or more way process between individuals. No one individual owns the friendship or has rights over it, over and above anyone else in the friendship group. No one individual should feel anger, hurt or jealousy if others in the friendship group spend time together without them.

There are lots of reasons why we form friendships with different people – each one bringing something to the relationship that perhaps another person doesn't.

Friendships are diverse – and we cannot and should not extend our own expectations of ourselves onto others. Just because you might not dream of speaking to someone in a certain way or saying a certain something to them, this does not mean that we can or should expect the same of them – each person has their own ways and mannerisms.

You should not hold a friend back if they are moving forward within their lives – if you truly are a friend, then you should be one unconditionally. This doesn't mean that the one moving forward should necessarily leave the others behind. A friend is a friend – regardless of which level.

It's about accepting someone for who they are, unconditionally – and not trying to change them unless they request your help to change.

Please use this space to record your responses to any questions which are either posed in this chapter or which arise from it.

Questions:

How did this chapter make you feel?

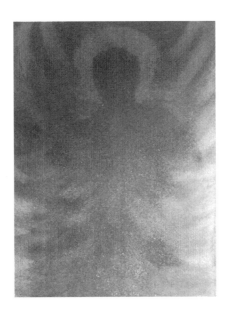

*I give permission to my higher being to take
control over what is the best route for me,
and to guide me to the best of my potential
on the earth plane.*

5. Boundaries and Control, and Controlling Boundaries

Boundaries are in everything: something we can put in place within all our lives, should we wish, as a boundary is something that we choose what acceptable to us and what is not. Every person's perception of this can be different.

We've talked about new relationships and patterns – but what is control, than a cycle of patterns?

So we're looking at controlling our boundaries in relationships. We control our boundaries, dependent upon whom we are with – we may show one aspect of ourselves to one person, and another aspect to someone else, and a whole range of other aspects to others. We are multi-faceted: mother, father, daughter, son, auntie, uncle, niece, nephew, best friend, colleague, lover, husband, wife, partner, mistress, counsellor, confidante, employer, employee, to name but a few.

Certain personality types will use control over a relationship in order to maintain control over their own selves.

If you were bullied at school, the bully may be acting in this way in order to prevent himself from being bullied. If you are in a healthy relationship with someone you share 50/50 in the control of the relationship, not with one person controlling the other.

There are different levels of control – financial ("don't spend that, that's your money, that's my money"), emotional control, sexual control.

This is applicable to both sexes and all relationships, not just romantic ones.

Control can be conscious as well as unconscious.

The conscious controller is afraid of losing some aspect / value of their life.

The unconscious controller could be repeating a pattern from previous relationships – either from childhood or other relationships – without realising it.

Self-control could include for example; designating yourself as the driver for the evening when out with friends, not having an alcoholic drink and maintaining safety for all.

The belief system can reach hidden depths in order for you to have self-control in your life.

So what is control?

Fear based control is a feeling of fear in response to a particular situation.

During our life trusting that you will be given whatever you want whenever you want it because we constantly try to control our lives – we go to work, we shop, we pay our bills – is that all fear based?

Not necessarily – but let's look back to childhood. As a little child you might need to go to the toilet but mummy says "hold it till we get to a toilet". This teaches self-control of the body, regulating the bladder, then regulating emotions, controlling your own temper… Control is consequential action. If you didn't control your bladder, you would wet yourself.

Take, for example, the adult fetish of wearing nappies and paying someone to take control as a "parental" figure. This is where someone wishes to have control taken from them – being submissive to the dominant parental figure. However, the adult in the nappy is actually in control, as he is paying for the situation to take place!

Take the woman in the supermarket – her child wants something, she says no, the child cries, the woman gets angry for she feels everyone is watching – people may be embarrassed, or judge the woman or the child. We are conditioned to see things in different ways. The child is purely exhibiting a pattern of behaviour, thus promoting a learning of the parental boundaries.

Take the child who is told "no, don't do that, that's naughty" when they are touching something – what do they learn? That being inquisitive about their surroundings is wrong. Developmentally, it is good to teach boundaries to a child – but when does the line get crossed?

What is a boundary?

A boundary is a limitation – and what is acceptable to you. We impose these on children, who grows up with a set of limitations – when fundamentally there should not be any limits on a child's upbringing.

The world does not stop revolving if you take a day off from control. What are you controlling, and what can you let go of?

We all need boundaries of some sorts within our lives, but we do not need to be held down by them all the time.

We learn the value of money by buying what we can afford. That's a big form of control – some people massively overspend, others scrimp and save. It starts from parental control about the value of money. This is learnt sometimes by how much the parent earns, and how much free money they have within the household. Some can feel guilty about being out at work all day so they overspend on the child – but is that guilt? Not a form of control?

What's the difference?

We can reward a child for doing something well, but it doesn't have to be hugely expensive. Are we taking control of the guilt to mask our feelings of inadequacy?

Back to romance.....

If a person finds themselves in a relationship where the other person is controlling them, and they wish to change their situation they may finds themselves feeling afraid. Acknowledging firstly that there is a self-destructive element of control which is self-destructive.

Emotional blackmail pertaining to guilt, transforms into control – the partner says "I can't live without you, I'll commit suicide if you go". This may be harsh and often said in the heat of the moment in a desperate attempt to maintain control of the relationship.

Spiritually, is this just ego running rampant within the body, taking control? Or is it the human aspect, when being out of control takes over the day to day running's of their life. Freedom vs imprisonment? Are we our own jail keepers?

If we are almost imprisoned by a partner, our soul is restricted in our body. But we are our own jail keepers and we have free will, unless we choose to be controlled, should we wish to, and whatever kind of relationship we wish to be in.

Who benefits from the "Fifty Shades of Grey" relationship? As consenting adults, both would benefit for a control /release relationship. As long as you are a consenting participant in all activities within your relationship. Are you then allowing yourself to take control of personal responsibility of your own control?

Deep down, we all know our own levels of how much we want to be controlled, and how much we are controlled. Mass media mind control plays into this – we are told what we should look like, what we should buy, where we should go, etc.

At some point in your life you will give way to control as it is easier to let somebody else take control. You might employ a Personal Assistant because you don't want to – or don't have time for – doing the tasks that need doing. You choose your battles, you choose what to control. With a child, you give them tasks to do at home, like load the dishwasher – but in some cases it can feel too difficult to control them in this way.

How much energy do you use in controlling your environment, and do you get that energy back?

There are many aspects of control within a marriage.

For example; controlling when the groom can see the dress – only on the day, see the bride on the wedding day – not until the wedding, the wedding is paid by the bride's family, the dress is white, there is an aisle (i.e. a church is involved), extended family attending but you can't sit Uncle Mick next to Auntie Sally, etc.

Please use this space to record your responses to any questions which are either posed in this chapter or which arise from it.

Questions:

How did this chapter make you feel?

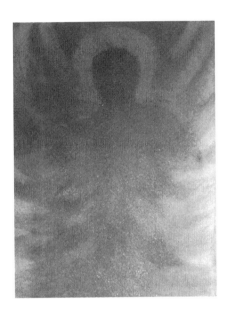

Your vessel will speak its mind.

Listen and begin to maintain a more healthier body.

6.   The human scale

"The human vehicle is the soul's marionette": Annette Moss

Our higher being is the puppeteer of everything that we do. Within the puppetry, emotions can surface.

There are some people who are angry – not just within themselves but with the whole world.

Anger at self and life. From a male perspective, I've experienced anger around myself and my situation and have had a lot of male students with anger, and trying to deal with it. It's destructive to their own being.

What is it about being a man that makes this anger so big? Genetic? The way we were brought up?

Is it the primitive hereditary level of going out as cavemen to fight animals and each other?

The scale can go up through the chakra system perhaps?

Anger is red. What does seeing red promote? Fight and flight. Survival instinct.

Is anger and frustration part of your survival instinct? It's a very powerful emotion keeping us alive.

The ego is the base, it keeps it alive. Embracing anger in the right way is the point – making it constructive anger, channelling it to promote change. The energy of anger, if it can be moved up through the body into consciousness, it can sustain us.

So if we move up to the sacral – then we have orange. Orange and red blend. Then the solar plexus – yellow – this blends further.

What about the victim – the person who always sees themselves as the victim. The poor me syndrome, I can't get out of this, it is always happening to me. This is an absence of will, will power. I keep trying this or that, but it's not enough. Why aren't I enough. It's personality.

Being hot-headed is reactive, temper, frustration, breaking point, triggers. Knowing your own breaking point is key – this allows control. Anger needs to be controlled.

Orange – sacral – moving the anger into creative, directing the sense of power, where am I going to put it, how am I going to deal with this anger. Some people use this in a creative or an athletic way, competition.

The Greeks made competition a sport – early civilisations have competition at the core. Same with animals – the biggest most ferocious lions gets the females.

Does competition sit well with the soul and with spirituality? I see it as a sense of achievement – we are competing against ourselves, where we are our own worst enemy. This is how the best athletes become the best – they are constantly trying to better their personal bests.

In that sense, it is a spiritual goal – we as spiritual beings want to be the best we can be.

Is your personal best your goal? Have you done the best you can?

As a spiritual being, do you set your own personal best before you enter the body? Not just in relationships, this can be in every part of your life.

You are the only person that can say you have done your best. You know this. You are your own executioner.

Back to the scale – creativity moves into the heart, intellectual, fear.

Fear – the victim is fearful – which leads us into the personality type.

If you have a being of consciousness, a soul, it incarnates into a body which develops – is the soul devoid of personality?

As a spiritual being, your soul personality will influence the human personality in how we move forward.

It is this influence which can create conflict. But our soul personality is off the scale in comparison with what the human personality can imagine.

Your soul personality may well be 95% asleep in the human incarnation. It would be too much for the human host to deal with the whole, it would be a useless life.

So soul amnesia is important. Certain parts come through – déjà vu, for example – to remind us of our purpose and to steer the human back on course.

We can't really talk about the soul personality much more as it is out of our perception. It is an influence – but to some it is inconsequential as they oblivious, it's outside of their bubble.

If you were 75% spiritual personality, you would not be able to maintain relationships or a job – you wouldn't have a care about all this, you would be beyond all of this.

It's an illusion.

For a really conscious being, it is recognising that everything is an illusion, but still you are in the play and you are learning. And until you are reach the final act, you are in the play of your life.

At what point do you exit? That would be the heart centre. You can be up in your heart and off planet – head being clairvoyance, cram, open to everything, at one with the world and the world is at one with you – but the heart centre is where you can go up and feed from the top, and down and feed from there.

The heart centre is the ego. The id is at the top, then the superego.

This is who you are, your body energy centres. Then at what point do you look at the body, when we talked about the body speaking its mind – what is taking control in us?

We need to bring our ego forward, this is fundamentally important, I want to do this but can't.

Which leads back to self-esteem and confidence and wanting to reclaim control, empowering yourself.

A reminder of who you are and your love for yourself: when you say "come back to centre" and you start to draw that energy back in and look at it – what does this really mean? Why have I let myself, the esteem, go?

I'm on my steam train, it's run out of steam, I can't get to the next stop. The steam train needs fuel to go into it to allow it to keep going up the track. So at what point do you get off at the next stop, take a look around and see what is there?

That's where the heart can be the central place to bring you back up and say "yes you are worth it, you have been in the base too much" – then you go up further and that's where you are speaking your truth.

Speaking your truth from the heart centre is kindness. From the base is anger and need. The heart is where you speak your truth.

Then go to the third eye where you can visualise the life that you want – imagination, which can be anything, imagining what you want or what you don't want, your thought process.

In the realms of imagination you are tapping into the soul history, the memory bank of where you have been – because the life you are in is just one lifetime. And how you are mirroring your life at any one given time because you are looking at a different perspective.

Your choice may be different in another life – it's a choice reaction, promoting change in the chain.

How we feel affects everything – we are all connected to the one, the monad – that's when you have to start saying that our collective feeds back into the one head source, our monad.

Any time in our particular lifetime, the lessons filter back to the source of our creation – our source monad – which has all these different lessons from the various lives we have been living – then the monad allows us to tap into this to push ourselves in the life where you might be struggling.

The crown is our connection to the divine – the god head. This is our clairvoyance, mediumship communication, with our self, our higher self, angelic being, the universe, god, to whatever we define god as, everything we find sacred, our divinity of our god. This would come down into the throat chakra and into the heart – this is how we feel love and interpret love from our source.

This goes back to previous conversation on "Do we need the force of the god head to feel love? I love therefore I am a believer…"

This takes me to making contact with people's loved ones, feeling a sense of love from these beings – a return to love, to that energy. Bringing down from the crown chakra so that we can speak, into the heart, so we can speak the love that we channel from source.

It doesn't matter what we believe the source is – it is OUR source for creation, not someone else's. If we believe in a source it is the universal creator for us.

The only person who can change what we feel about this is by being openminded, to allow other people to express their religious beliefs, showing that you are a spiritual being, allowing others to be themselves, showing spiritual maturity.

It's not accountable by human age, it's by soul age.

Please use this space to record your responses to any questions which are either posed in this chapter or which arise from it.

Questions:

How did this chapter make you feel?

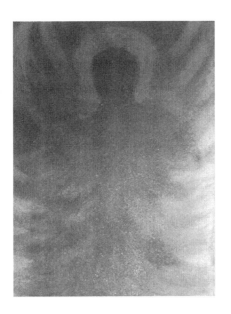

*Confidence in you own abilities is believing
you have the power to drive yourself
forwards.*

7.   Spirituality and sexuality

There are different levels of being sexual with someone – different levels of sex.

Lust for the body

Lust for a specific need to be fulfilled

For this chapter we are talking more about how to build a loving relationship between two consensual beings and bringing sensual into the relationship – this might not even involve penetration, it can mean heightened energy to reach a climatic end, which could last for hours, a blending of energy.

This is very similar to the basis of tantric sex.

A loving relationship between two consenting people wanting to develop their sexual relationship to a new level, to really get absorbed in the actual act of sex.

For many people, sex is a goal agenda – a man goes into the sexual situation because he wants to have an orgasm or a woman wants to please him – she has been brought up to believe that once he has an orgasm and is pleased, she is pleased and they can both rest.

Is that sexual fulfilment? It is a momentary fulfilment of a desire, an orgasmic desire – yes, you can go anywhere and be pleasured both for men and women – but a women can be truly pleasured by having multiple orgasms that last for hours, unlike the solitary orgasm that most men can have. It's about being the partners who can put the energy of their self into satisfying the other – raising your energy enough to give your partner the heightened ecstasy. It's the same for same-sex relationships – they need to give each other the time. We're not talking simply about physiological changes to the body – we're talking about energy exchange. Physiologically, there's a release of endorphins which last a few hours – but via energy it can last for much longer.

An exercise: Raise the energy with your partner, to a certain vibration but don't take it further – keep it there for a length of time – and THEN go to the next level together.

For women, the energy that you feel in your loins is energy building up. likewise for a man, it is about delaying orgasm to become more in tune with the woman. This can result in both having a longer orgasm, is keeps building, then stopping, then building, then stops, then building further.

Maintaining the cosmic orgasm – taking it to the next level where you can quite easily leave your body / bodies (both of you) to experience something so beautiful, beyond orgasm – this is making love with the soul – soul to soul entanglement. Blending the energies of a physical orgasm, raising the vibrations between you, then it becomes beyond the physical.

If you are not in the right relationship to explore beyond the physical orgasm, then for many people they will not experience this. And that's fine – but if you are with your partner and you want to experience a deeper connection, you can try this. Equally, you can self-satisfy by doing this on your own, raising your own energies and even reach orgasm without physical touch.

Your relationship with yourself should be the first and main relationship. How to pleasure yourself is not just physical but energetic. Hold your hand an inch or so away from your body – scan your body – feel the energies – see how it makes you feel.

Sexual relationships might not just be with one partner but with multiple partners – as long as it's consenting, then that's fine. But to develop a fulfilling relationship, the most sacred sex act, can take time to find. You need to be in a supportive relationship here.

It's about blending each other's lifeforces, fluids – whether it be the hormonal woman in her monthly flow, it's sharing the energy – and that the body is a playground.

The "play" word is important – sex should be playful, an exploration of each other – and that might never end.

How we feel from one day to another should feel different all the time towards our partner.

Be creative, be experimental if you both choose to. This is a sure-fire way to keep your relationship hot and happy.

But if you find you are not in a loving relationship, be as authentic as possible in the relationships in which you find yourself. The most important part is to be authentic to yourself.

If, after orgasm, men can still build the sexual energy, they can reach fulfilment.

Simmering sexual energy to reach the cosmic orgasm. Anyone can do this, in whatever relationship – on their own, with someone else.

The sexual cosmic orgasm is not defined by sexual orientation or gender.

It's not conditional, there are no conditions to blending energies as long as you enjoy the energy you are blending with – this is the most important part.

If you experience any medical issues or psychological problems during sexual intercourse, please contact your doctor. No problem is too big or too small – and usually they are likely to have heard it all before from prior patients, so don't feel embarrassed about discussing a personal issue.

Talking about the heart and the head, for men, a lot of sexual relationships are held in the head – it doesn't matter if he has an erection or not, he can still have tantalising sexual thought that could allow sexual relationship with the partner. Sex doesn't have to be all one-sided, me me me. Blending energies is key – it's not about sexual fulfilment. Love making is based on energy – and how much energy you put in is what you will get out of it. And it is sacred – sexuality is sacred.

Sometimes you might find as a spiritual sexual being you may have wet dreams, dreaming you have sex with someone else. Your spiritual being has left your body and is having sex elsewhere on an astral plane. This is astral sex.

So, if you are in a relationship, and you are asleep – and you have astral sex during your sleep – are you cheating? Any person, spiritual or not, can wake up with lustful feelings – does this mean you have had astral sex during your sleep? If you are consciously aware that you are going to the astral plane for sex then this is cheating.

Many people fantasise during sex with their partner – as they are not being aroused so are either arousing their mind with a fantasy person – or they are not being aroused at all and the relationship is a failure. If the relationship isn't meeting it's sexual desire, and you find that you are distracting your mind with an outside source, this needs addressing to find out what's going on – talking to your partner.

It's about taking control of your own being and deciding whether you are in a committed relationship or would be better off not committed to one particular being. You are able to do what you please. You may decide you like both sexes so it doesn't matter which one you sleep with, it's about the energy and personal responsibility. But if you are hurting somebody else, that takes it into the realm of cheating. You have to be open and honest in your relationship but you have to be open and honest with yourself first.

If you are engaging consensually in group sexual activities, then you are blending with lots of other energies who have also blended with lots of other energies – so you are effectively sexually engaging with everyone they have previously been with. It's about sexually transmitted energies NOT just sexually transmitted diseases.

If you are embarking on a new relationship with anyone, it is also wise to disconnect from previous partners – so send an energetic "cutting" to that person so that whoever they sleep with in future will not have a connection with your energy.

You could bring these into Succubus and Incubus into your relationship, so it is important to cleanse you own sexual field – but also that of your partner, if they are willing. This can be done by an energy clearing visualisation, or ask their higher self for permission to do it if they are not spiritually open enough to do it.

This really does reinforce energetic sex.

This allows you to clear from sexual transmitted diseases as well as the energy that the new partner has been carrying.

If you are consciously aware that you are raising your sexual vibrations together in a loving relationship be mindful that it is your relationship and that no other energy is going to come in and use that energy.

Spiritual orgy is where other energies come in to witness and indulge on the sexual energy between the two people. This is something to be mindful of – others surfing the sexual orgasmic wave.

Don't forget – we were given the human body to be used in whichever way we wish to use it, and with whomever as a consenting adult.

If you have something like the incubus or succubus in your relationship – can they influence you to behave in a certain sexual way that you wouldn't normally behave? And therefore that's when you would hopefully question what is going on with you – why have you all of a sudden changed the way that you act?

What about the person who claims that their spiritual being made them act in a particular way in regards to sex?

They could claim to being influenced by something externally which is referred to as overshadowing. Some people feel more comfortable to blame their behaviour on someone else's actions or on another situation.

Overshadowing can come into mediumship, relationship, with regard to food, etc. You could easily have somebody very strong in nature that still feels that they want to drink alcohol, eating, smoke, have sex – and use somebody susceptible and influence that person to get off on having a drink, eating, smoking, having sex, etc.

Being influenced by spiritual energies has been in our civilisation from the very beginning.

We have deliberately chosen not to include some taboo subjects in this book, because we are not here to name and shame or to judge – we are non-judgemental spiritual beings.

Please use this space to record your responses to any questions which are either posed in this chapter or which arise from it.

Questions:

How did this chapter make you feel?

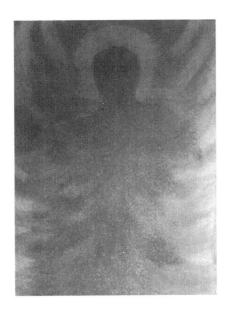

When the dark comes calling ...

Turn up your light and dispel it...

*Send it back to the shadows or embrace it
with love and light...*

*Either way, stand in your own power and
light the way for others.*

8.   Choices

When the ultimatum really isn't an ultimatum as we have a choice to decide – but in reality we don't have to make a decisions, none is better. Love is still love, and love makes you feel good from the heart so you shouldn't have to make a decision on whether to work on something with someone you love – neither should be made to choose.

It's all judgement at the end of the day.

Common saying – the head or the heart – what does this mean? The head is the mind, thought, thinking about things – this takes time – "I need time."

Whereas the heart should be an immediate response as you feel it – ultimately we should always go with the heart – but we are used to going to the head.

When it comes to a loving relationship – the question is love or lust – love comes from the heart, because you feel it – but lust / desire comes also. Is it the desire to be loved? Do we mistake lust for love because we desire to be loved?

With lust, it's desire – it's my needs, what can I get now. Desire is about cravings.

Searching for the job that you would love to work in – this will certainly feed the earning of the money and love of the job and how long you need to be in that job role – but equally it needs to be met by the head – the work relationship needs to be intellectual to keep you stimulated.

If you're not stimulated in a relationship that's where you can become bored – one person might want to talk football, the other trainspotting. You could be a spiritual person in a relationship where there's no spirituality or no shared spiritually. Different sides of a coin – who is giving love? The spiritual being is then becoming more humanised if the partner is not of the same persuasion.

For a relationship to develop, you need the mind connection. Once the initial fireworks – the honeymoon period – die down, come off the boil, then you are left with the companionship, and need to establish what you have got in common. This should always be the substance of the relationships – the meeting of souls, then minds, then bodies.

When the body relationship goes you should have the mind and the soul connection remaining until you talk yourself out of the relationship (that's the mind at work there). That's where the love and lust come in – you desire someone, fancy the pants off them, go into a relationship that's built on sexual desire, on what you see physically about somebody else.

It says a lot for meeting on the internet where you don't actually see the person – you write letters / love letters, you get to know that person. The letters are written from the heart – then you meet. By that point you have probably fallen in love with the character of the person, their personality. That's when disappointment can come in as you have fantasised about what this person will look like, not just aesthetically but physically.

The soul connection in the relationship, where the love grows because you feel it from the instant – it's not really love at first sight, it's the soul connection that ignites the flame and love can start to build, then simmer, and grow, and then boil – and you can keep it boiling as you have built up that relationship.

So what happens when the mind isn't met?

That's when you reach out in conversation with others and your attention goes elsewhere – and it's not that you want to be out of the relationship that you are in, it's that it doesn't meet you on all levels. And sometimes that works as you have a healthy relationship with your partner and you are together as you enjoy each other's company. Not all relationships meet on all levels.

Having things in common can cover gaps where they don't meet. This changes the relationship.

Take one party out, let them have a weekend away separately, then meet up again – spending time apart can increase the relationship connection.

It's nice to have things outside of the relationship – and work is predominantly one of these things. For many couples, this is how it is.

If a person does the same thing as their partner, they will often stop talking about work as there is no need to discuss something they both know. So at what point does the overlap of work come into the home and affect the relationship? You could have a constant talk of work – if you have work / life sorted, then you have eight hours at work plus travel time, overtime and your work / home ratio is off, so there's something you need to address to have a balance.

Balance needs to be addressed in our lives.

When you look at the spiritual aspect, you don't want to be confined in a job role that grounds you – you have to go to work to make the money to do what you want to do – it's a vicious circle.

For someone with fewer responsibilities, they can give up their work and do what they want – this comes back to choice.

At what point do you choose the life that you live? Is it a conscious decision or something that you make from the heart or the head?

That brings us back to the centre again – starting with choice, ending with a choice.

Exercise:

Get a magazine.

Cut out images from the magazine of things that you want in your life.

Then create a plan on how you are going to get them.

If you want to be a size 12 in your clothing, take an image of a size 12 model, and add a photo of your head to it – then stick it on your fridge door. Every time you go to pick out something to eat, look at the image. Surround it with positive words – "beautiful", "elegant", "happy", "comfortable" etc.

It doesn't have to be size related, it can be anything that you want – a handbag, a holiday, a house, a particular job, a book, a life style.

Picture it, picture yourself having it.

How are you going to get there? Make a plan, and go after it!

Please use this space to record your responses to any questions which are either posed in this chapter or which arise from it.

Questions:

How did this chapter make you feel?

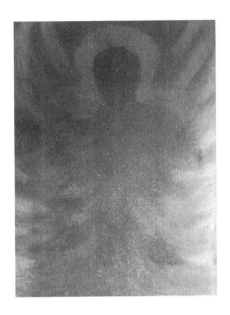

Memorabilia collected during one's lifetime,
represent our most treasured thoughts....

We can't take those said possessions with
us, when depart this world...

What we do hold close to our hearts are the
memories of love...

Especially unconditional...

Live life and love eternal.

9. Spiritual detox when the human side doesn't want to

The collective waste that we hoard within our mind – the cathartic detoxification, how much of ourselves do we recycle?

Clearing out the corners of your mind where a defecation is required – effectively, clearing the shit out, to prevent it from infesting and affecting the rest of your wellbeing. How much does it cloud your reasoning, when a normal sane person becomes temporarily insane. This is where compartmentalising your information is key – how much information can you (and should you) retain on certain subjects that cause pain.

For a full detoxification of the body, a being would need to go "cold turkey", only ingesting natural products, no additives. To promote wellbeing, we use herbs and floral remedies. The body retains infection.

Why do we keep rage in its cage, when releasing it at an earlier point when it just annoys you, so it's almost stopping the rage from brewing – communication is important.

In adolescence, in men generally, it can be an issue for them to release anger. This also happens with some women, it should be said. Men usually see the way that their father reacts to their mother, and take this as their instruction on how to treat a woman.

Anger should be released as an emotional energy – it's about how we do it, and in what way. If it's released at a person, we're taking it out on someone. So how else can it be released in a non-hurtful manner, and subsequently without creating violence? And at what scale?

More often than not, holding onto hurt can result in high levels of anger – this needs talking through in relationships. Too many people are unable to discuss and argue, without becoming hostile, venomous, rageful or dangerous. Dealing with a situation with communication in order to resolve the emotions, via constructive feedback and discussion – if you have a problem expressing verbally, write it down: what is making you feel this way? Find a way to bring a calmer and more peaceful resolve from a situation. Learning your triggers towards anger and rage – we all have a trigger response. How long does it take for you to be triggered? How much can you be pushed, and how much will you allow yourself to be pushed before reaching breaking point?

As a non-confrontational being, it might take a while to reach your breaking point – you are open to the unconditional love of another person as you are a spiritual being. And when will you stand up and say "no more"? Stop playing the same record over and over until it's completely scratched and ruined, instead rewrite your own CD, your "control defence".

Please use this space to record your responses to any questions which are either posed in this chapter or which arise from it.

Questions:

How did this chapter make you feel?

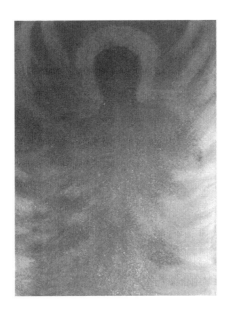

I watch you when you sleep....

I am with you when you're sad....

I feel your love for the future....

I embrace you when you cry....

I smile when you're happy....

I will always be with you....

*We met in spirit form, my wings enfold
you....*

My love for you is unconditional....

For I am your Guardian Angel xxxx

10. Forgiveness

Our memories are a storage of time – our experiences.

If you can revisit your past, would you change things? Would you change how you felt, and how you chose to remember something – by doing so, you may be able to forgive and change things.

Everyone's perception of a past event is liable to be different due to their thought processes during the event – their views can be clouded because of how they felt, whether this be anger, frustration, hurt or something else.

We are very harsh critics – of ourselves and others. We judge and compare ourselves to others, and our behaviours to theirs.

If we go into a memory and relive an event in time, in the now, bringing it up now, can you change how you felt and responded then?

We can change how we NOW feel about the situation from the past. By revisiting a painful experience, what benefit is in this for you?

And in the present time, is it as painful as it was then? You could be looking at it objectively from a third party view, rather than looking at it directly.

If you look at it from the visual perspective of watching a movie: look at yourself as one of the main characters in the movie. Look at how the main characters interacted – who raised their voices, who was upset, who showed which emotions, how do you think that another person felt in the situation – step into their role to see things from their perspective. This allows you to see the fuller picture. Maybe at the time, you thought you were being chastised for something – but were you in the wrong, or was that other person just trying to point across a point that you could not see at the time.

There are so many reasons why we have painful events and hold them within us – but by revisiting them and looking at them from another angle, we can change how we felt about it.

If you are not happy with a situation then revisiting it can help you to change your viewpoint of what happened.

The reason for doing this is to show how far you have come forward from then and have you learned from the pattern – or are you repeating the patterns from the first experience? At some point, you have to get off the Merry-Go-Round of always acting the same way to a situation.

Look at what was going on for you at that particular juncture in time – not just this one particular memory. What led to this point, what was happening in your life at this point that contributed or led to the situation? It could be a number of things that caused the avalanche to cascade down the mountain and gather momentum. Every argument has a starting point – something that sparks the flame. Was it something within YOU that was that spark, that you weren't feeling good about something within yourself, that set off the argument or contributed towards the situation?

Little things over a period of time can build up and suddenly it becomes a momentous explosion or a volcanic eruption.

It is always good to look back to the time leading up to the incident, to see the series of events that led up to the explosion.

Therefore revisiting a painful experience with the thought processes that we have now can help us to change it into a more positive experience as we have looked at it from a different perspective.

We can acknowledge that we are what we are today, because of how we lived then. We need to appreciate that whatever happened is part of our journey.

Is it of benefit to revisit the past to create a more positive future?

Yes, if you are willing to forgive and move on, the past can be looked at from a different perspective or viewpoint and with a different understanding. If you are willing to desensitise the experience and withhold judgement, only then can you promote an attitude of forgiveness to yourself and others.

This doesn't mean you are then being the victim and leaving yourself as such – you are allowing yourself to forgive and move forward, no longer the victim, promoting a more objective response. It's an empowerment of self.

Forgiving to move on

Forgiveness is a major element to being able to move forward with any difficult situation – and also with any conflict within ourselves.

It really is OK to give ourselves permission to forgive ourselves.

Forgiving yourself is the biggest thing you can do. If you can't forgive yourself, how can you expect or ask anyone else to?

Revisiting your past can be a painful experience.

Exercise: forgiving yourself and others

If it is yourself that you need to forgive, then the exercise of looking at yourself in the mirror and talking to yourself:

See yourself in the mirror, in the place you were in at the particular time of distress and look at your face. Look at how your present body is reacting to seeing your past body – look at how you are holding yourself and the emotions being displayed. Is your head being held high, to the side, down, have you got tears in your eyes – are you smiling or are you sad.

Look at the emotions being displayed. Talk to your past self saying "I'm sorry for causing you harm, pain or distress. It was a necessary experience and I'm grateful that you have allowed me to experience that."

Then look at your past self body and face starting to change. Is there a softening going on? A more vibrant look? Look at how the apology is reflected, and how you are starting to forgive yourself.

Allow the past self to talk to the present one: "yes, it was an experience I am glad I have had – and I would not now be able to look at the situation in this way, had you not moved forward within your life."

This exercise can be adapted as though you are looking at someone else in the mirror, to assist you in forgiving them.

It may be that they harmed you – or you harmed them – and you can say from one to the other "thank you for the lessons that this teaches us".

Next, look at the mirror and see your future self and say "thank you for helping me with forgiveness."

Your future self can then say back "well done, and thank you for promoting healing on this past situation – I now have moved forward and am still moving forward, with the knowledge that you have helped me to grow and understand what forgiveness is."

This exercise can be adapted to family timelines, to help promote healing with family rifts.

This changes the energy of that timeline to forgiveness – the act of forgiveness can promote a positive energy change that can hopefully promote wellbeing in our future lives.

Please use this space to record your responses to any questions which are either posed in this chapter or which arise from it.

Questions:

How did this chapter make you feel?

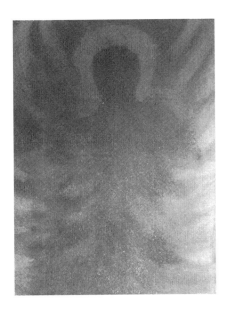

Ride the wave of creativity.

Live in the tides of life.

Dance in the puddle of emotion.

Love every season and shed only tears of joy.

11. Time

How much time do we have on the planet, when time in the spirit world is linear?

Very much on the earth planet, time is important. Our daily lives are set to a timescale – we get up at a certain, we start work at a time, we finish at a time. The media – television and entertainment systems are all related to time.

Time limits us and binds us to the physical – in our distant past, our only way to measure the passage of time was by the movement of the sun and moon, the tides of the ocean, and the changing of the seasons – particularly for sowing and harvesting crops.

In the spiritual world, time is not important – this is a human measurement or conditioning.

Individual perceptions of time may vary – time may 'feel' fast or slow for any given moment for a particular person – but the astronomical clock and the nuclear clocks of scientists will tell us that time has continued at its normal rate.

What happens in time doesn't allow us to measure what's out of time.

For spiritual beings, we are now talking 'beyond time'.

A nomadic person, for instance, would not adhere to time – they would sleep when they feel like it, get up when they feel like it, they would eat when hungry – they do not adhere to a particular clock other than day to day, existing in their own world within a world. 'Time' for them exists within their own world

To interact with the rest of the world around them, they would need to react to its time constraints, so in a sense, their own perception of time is subjective.

We all feel at some point during our lifetime, a fear of mortality. A constant knowing that death is close.

Death and life are the same thing – to live is the same as to die. Both should be embraced. Death is a constant, the duality of life. Putting one off, stops us from truly embracing the other. Our fear of death could prevent us from fully enjoying life. Hence thinking "I don't want to take a risk for something because it could cause harm".

What keeps you in a job that you are unhappy with? Ultimately the fear of death is at the end of the trail of no money, no house, no food, no life. Fear of losing people, losing yourself, losing accumulated possessions.

The one thing we all have in common is that we are all born and we all die – how we live in between is down to us individually. We own nothing, we have brought nothing with us at birth, and we take nothing with us. What we can leave is our mark, a legacy, what we did with our existence.

This is about the time of your life – making the most of your time here and not living in fear of dying, because that is inevitable. So enjoy the journey – this is your journey! The conclusion is death – and then re-joining our Monad in the spirit world to integrate our knowledge to our own collective.

A person might say "I'm finally doing what I want to do, and have been doing for the last two years, I have a list of things I want to do from now onwards, what if I don't have enough time? I have a need to do certain things before I die. I'm not ready to go yet."

Another might say "I've made a mark that's important to me, I have contributed to the earth and to other people, I am not afraid of dying."

Another might see a nomad sitting by the side of the road begging, and think "I'm not going to be like that, I'm going to work hard and pay my mortgage so I don't have to be in that situation."

There is so much busy-ness in our lives that we fill our time – how often have you said "I haven't had time to do this or that"?

We need to take time out for holiday, to wind down, to slow the busy-ness of the brain.

Go back a hundred years or more to times of manual labour for a much bigger percentage of the population – they worked harder, working the body to death. Now, we work, we have entertainment, pollution, environment, different stresses and strains on our time – we are pulled in more directions and don't find a balance, which leads to stress and illness and death. We manage our time very differently than we used to. It's not taught in school. Nor is stress management.

School teaches playtime, lunchtime, work time – then we move forward to deadlines. Note the word "dead" in "deadlines", as opposed to "lifeline". Then we reach retirement age and then that's the end of time for the person.

If we knew when we were going to die – how does that change things? If given a healthy death-date (i.e. you are a healthy being) and then were given a death date, would that change how you use your time? Note: we are not talking here about having a terminal illness, where you are given a timescale for death but you are not able to utilise the time you have left due to the inhibitions of your illness.

Procrastination is what we do when we put up barriers to doing things. Time procrastination is what we do because we place different levels of importance on things that we do – what is important to us, as opposed to important because of others, job, house, time, relationship. Taking control of your own time, because you are important, is important.

If you do something but don't want to or are doing it out of guilt, that's not doing it unconditionally.

You can't rewind time – you can't turn back the clock, but you can wind it up again or put new batteries in it and move forward with momentum.

We can then tap into our past lives and move forwards into our future lives – as they are all running alongside each other.

Have you ever experienced déjà vu? This perhaps explains why, as you perhaps have already experienced something in a previous life which you are now re-experiencing and recognising even though it is "new" in this life.

Please use this space to record your responses to any questions which are either posed in this chapter or which arise from it.

Questions:

How did this chapter make you feel?

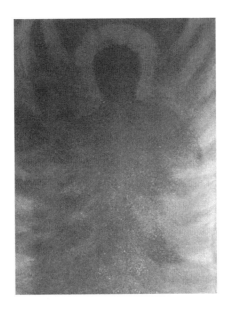

Once you see yourself as an individual,

and start to think of yourself as an equal amongst others,

it is only then that you can begin to see

and realise your own worth.

12. The Goddess

The principal of this chapter is in this life, a woman (before her own birth) may choose whether to have a child or not.

Some women may find that, whilst they choose that they want to be a mother, they can't for one reason or another. Others, who choose not to have children, may find themselves in the situation of being pregnant.

Regardless, each woman will go through the menopausal stage – some might sail through it and for others it might hinder their life.

For this chapter, we are looking at being a mother.

Healing the birth canal

A woman can heal herself after having a child, to then move into a new phase of relating to her partner and her children. If she has a difficult birth, she can possibly hold on to negative energies about the birth in her relationships with the child.

Healing the birth canal promotes not just a physical but also a spiritual connecting to relationships – whether this be the child or adult relationships, male or female – whoever your partner is.

Healing the birth canal, even if a woman has not given birth, shows that it is ok not to give birth in this life, but to also embrace the physical sexual goddess as well as the mother goddess.

Reading up spiritual issues around the holy grail vesical piscis (the overlapping area in the two circles image below)

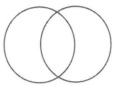

– the spiritual cup of life, the vessel that echoes the shape of the female womb, the energy of creation – all women are goddesses because they have the power of creation in themselves. Women by their birth right are goddesses, whether they create life or not, but can still use that energy to create things.

Some women may find that, by being with a man, he may be there specifically within the relationship to birth a child. As the woman gets older and goes through the menopause, she will no longer be fertile and the "empty nest syndrome" can come into play – and may bring new energy forward with another new partner with children to play and create a new woman in herself.

Are we saying – there is healing to be done, you need to go and do it, and how do you heal the birth canal?

We're giving thanks to the womb and the vagina for their place in creation and the pleasure found within the procreation act and experience, and for the creativity – and raising the kundalini energy. We are sexually birthed beings, all of us – so we have to get in contact with that part of ourselves, as otherwise it would not be being expressed in the most beneficial way for the body. Energy which is not released properly can get blocked – and if it gets blocked in the vagina, that can lead to problems in the ovaries, bladder, kidneys, and so on.

When you meet the partner who his able to help you in the healing process, or you can do it yourself – to release that energy, the fluid of the cup, this promotes a wellbeing, the sustainable, the love juice.

If a relationship is to develop in this arena, a partner who can be fully part of the experience, a mutual healing, is vitally important.

From a male perspective, a man holds onto patterns from past relationships and needs to work on this in order to be able to help their new partner in her healing.

The saying "you bring the woman out in me" says that you can bring out the sexual goddess.

It's been said that women who have an orgasm with a partner whom they truly love, it changes their body – their skin lights up, their eyes shine, they walk lighter on the earth for a couple of days afterwards.

But a woman can't get to the point of truly letting go with her partner if she is not feeling the love of her partner. It can be painful – as can the process the birth.

The body can change during birth – the vagina can loosen, or tighten up, or change in other ways – that make the woman feel she is NOT a goddess and does not want to be looked at or touched. This is where healing is paramount for future sexual relationships, whether they be alone or with someone else.

If you have felt like this as a woman, maybe you could ask your partner to help you through the healing stage.

Equally, for partners who watch their wife / girlfriend give birth, this can put them off sexual encounters with them afterwards – as they have now seen the woman as a mother goddess not a sexual goddess.

All of this needs healing to take us closer to the source, raising our energies together. The first thing to do is to talk with your partner or a counsellor or doctor – someone who will listen and can help you to understand what is going on with your body – or your partners' body. Not forgetting that it IS just a body while we are spirit – but this body gives you so much pleasure in eating, being, sleeping, everything – it is quite a huge part in our lives to say "thank you for this body".

So whether you have had a good or bad experience with the womb and those areas, give thanks for it, allow healing and allow the goddess to come through in order to move forward.

Some men have found it impossible to deal with their partner after she has given birth, as the sensations have changed due to the birth canal no longer feeling as it did pre-birth. For the man, this can take the attention away from him and he may feel inadequate or jealous of the child that has come into the world and made this change come about in the female.

This trauma will also affect the woman.

Later, both the woman and her male partner – go through the menopausal stage.

So we're talking about loving yourself, loving your partner, loving your bodies, loving each other – both before and after birth. There may be drugs, epidurals, forceps, long labour, C-section – all of these are layers of damage done to the woman's body. Afterwards, the trauma of this may be too much for some women who then struggle in their way in motherhood as they cannot accept their new body shapes.

Miscarrying a child can bring about anger at the inner being, that the body could not hold on to the child, and can cause huge problems.

Abortion can similarly cause difficulties on many levels – there's a huge healing process that needs to take place afterwards, no matter why the termination took place.

What happens from the male perspective after his partner gives birth?

Her insides and outsides may well have changed, she has new priorities, she is side-lined – she might not want to engage in sexual activities as she is too tired and otherwise engaged with motherhood or is still recovering from the birth. Plus the thought of having another child might be form of birth control for both parties as they both abstain from sex. This can have a lasting impression on either or both partners!

This is the time for unconditional love to come to the forefront – you are creating a family unit with each other, there should be no guilt laid at the feet of either partner for being tired or unable or not wanting or not feeling like it or for anything else that the trauma of birth might bring up.

This is where we can look at our own inner child and our own birth – how our parents embraced our birth, or otherwise.

For new parents, there can be a feeling of sheer terror of how to look after and be responsible for a new life. Bonding plays an enormous part in alleviating this terror, to bring the parent and child together. The child may not spiritually have wanted to be birthed – and the parent may not have wanted to have a child – or the child came into the world because the parents thought that having a child would solve their problems. All of these are issues that need a lot of healing.

Communication – good, open communication – between parents is crucial in moving forwards.

Please use this space to record your responses to any questions which are either posed in this chapter or which arise from it.

Questions:

ow did this chapter make you feel?

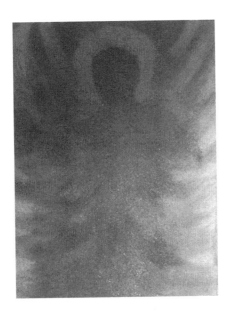

It is not always what we perceive —

is it much more for the observant

than the thinker?

13. Children – relationship with your child giving them space to grow

Before birth, we allow ourselves to disconnect from our spiritual memories. This is called 'voluntary amnesia' because spiritually speaking, a human child has everything that it needs when it is born. The child has a wealth of knowledge in its spiritual bank that, as they grow, can become known through the memory sprinkler process.

Your children are an extension of you. They are not you and therefore should be treated as individuals, and respecting their individuality is paramount for their growth.

In another chapter we talk about the spirit choosing to incarnate in the human body and your child's spirit may be a wise old soul, an evolved soul, in fact more evolved than yourself.

In that particular life, you choose your parents also and the life you are going to lead. Also before your parents are born, they talk to you and choose you, and you decide together to formulate the relationship that you are going to have so in some degree you already know your parents before you are born and you have made a decision to nurture or not the child.

You may only be wanting to facilitate the womb to give birth and to therefore give another parent the opportunity to bring your child up in to adulthood.

Or you may only choose to have the child in the womb for a very short period of time to experience this and then go back to spirit, on the understanding that it was never meant to be born and that it chose you as a parent to be their mother for that short period of time.

For this chapter, we are looking at parents bringing children in to the world and nurturing them and allowing them to learn and grow and mix with other children and adults in a social network so that as they grow they become socially mature within a community. They may then decide that they are going to a boarding school and therefore move away from home to study, they may have home schooling, they may go to school and play truant. You are not responsible for what the child does or doesn't do in their educational process – this is the spiritual framework. In the human, the parent is penalised for what the child might do.

Can you be with your child 24/7 when they are 14 or 15 years old, for example? You have to trust that your child is then walking the path of independence but that they are walking the right path, not stealing, doing drugs, drinking alcohol – self-sabotaging. You need your child to learn how to self-regulate, not self-sabotage.

Being a hands-on parent is not a job to take lightly.

Some parents have children and their career is important for social standing and environment – and this needs them to go to full-time work, and the child is put into a nursery environment. So therefore the child could be seen as being brought up by the care system – as in nursery, pre-school, school – a teaching environment in which we hope that they are learning social and environmental skills.

There are schools dotted around the world which provide an alternative education curriculum whilst focusing more on sociability, spirituality, environmental awareness, meditation from a very early age, and the skills to function within this world, rather than purely academic skills which satisfy our existing educational system's 'norms', where the better we are deemed to be at something, the better the job we can attain.

You can walk by the side of your child, but not be your child. You need to know and recognise your impact on their growth. If you recognise yourself as a spiritual being, are you better equipped to encourage your child to explore their spirituality – as the child starts to grow up, they start to question things about themselves in the bigger picture.

How to nurture a spiritual child – your rainbow and crystal children

If you acknowledge yourself as a spiritual being and therefore act as a spiritual parent, does this aid and benefit your child when your child has more human traits than the spiritual, or has chosen to actively rebel against their spiritual side?

One reason for rebelling could be that the parent hasn't spent much time with that child, letting them have the active care and attention from them that the child wants (note: not needs), but as a spiritual being the parent has instead allowed them to learn personal responsibility for themselves.

You plant seeds in a garden for them to grow and bloom into their best potential. Alternatively you can metaphorically plant a sensory garden where the child grows from the seeds that you plant and nurture: everything that they need to sustain a happy balanced life (smell, touch, taste, etc). Not forgetting, of course, the water feature within the garden to allow your child to develop their emotional growth.

Please use this space to record your responses to any questions which are either posed in this chapter or which arise from it.

Questions:

How did this chapter make you feel?

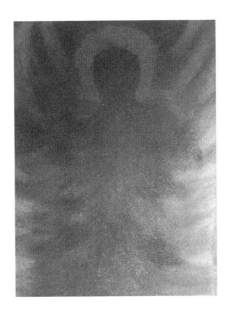

A fairy blessing is to kiss in the air.

Allow your breath to gently spread your wings

and fly towards your destination

with guidance from the elementals.

14. Logical questioning and our quest for knowledge – what is our instruction for life?

As a spiritual seeker you may find yourself asking questions all your life.

You will always find more questions – and there are as many questions as there are answers. Equally, there can be far more answers to any one question. Ultimately, you will only be able to work towards finding an answer when you start questioning.

You don't have to be spiritual to ask questions, but the spiritual seeker will ask the questions that go beyond the physical.

There are a list of questions which Mark and I would like you to consider in the following pages. With each, we invite you to add your own answers, as everybody's perceptions are different – after which we will give our perception of the answers.

Some questions we may never get the answers to in our lifetime, but sometimes is it enough to go with trust? You think it, therefore it is.

Perhaps you believe that there are worlds and beings and other planets, doorways to magical kingdoms.

The purpose of life can be seen as discovery so we ask questions – however, is the purpose of life actually about creation and creating ourselves?

We can have a million questions – but life is secret by its very nature and we are not meant to discover everything in one lifetime – and therefore are we not meant to know all the answers?

When we are born, we look to outside sources for our instruction – "you must not do this, you must do that". Our parents are the first instructors – we look outside ourselves for the first appreciation, the first words, the first reasons. Among the first words we usually learn are "yes" and "no".

As we then get older, at what point do we fully embrace our inner guide? We can put it off as long as we wish to, but it always needs to be done – we need to listen as the soul speaks to us. This is where personal responsibility follows.

So many people are taught to look within themselves to find an answer – the primary thing is to trust yourself. "I am responsible", not someone else.

We are all searching for answers.

Maybe in this life, we are not meant to remember that an aspect of our extended soul was present or may have been significant somewhere else at some other point in time in the earth's history, and therefore we may be trying to remember, in our fragmented human mind, that life which we had lived in the past.

Maybe we are shown it in dreams, sideways glances or as déjà vu, or outside our peripheral vision. Or – to throw a spanner in the works – maybe, just maybe, we are living in a parallel plane to the life that we are looking historically.

Maybe you are just asking questions about your life, your existence, your being – the eternal "who am I?"

Our minds can play tricks on us – we often remember what we want to remember. But our higher self knows all the answers to our questions.

As a human, we are much more fragmented in our questioning and answering capability.

Questions For You
(and space for your answers)

Was there really an Atlantis?

How were the pyramids made?

Why was Stonehenge built and why were stone circles positioned as they were?

What is the truth behind the myth of Jesus and Mary Magdalene's relationship?

Did the dinosaurs really become extinct because of a meteor or was there really a meteor?

The biggest question: who am I?

What is the purpose of the human life?

Answers from Annette and Mark...

Was there really an Atlantis?

Yes. We believe that the earth was created as a whole to be a place for many advanced planetary civilisations to use, in order to co-exist and to learn from. Each civilisation had a particular way of living.

Atlantis was created as an island in the Mediterranean, with civilisations who used telepathy as a form of communication.

They were non-judgemental and all worked together in harmony, many came in the human form and others came in their natural form as sentient animals that worked with and walked alongside the humans.

Inter-breeding between beings created new life forms including Minotaurs, Centaurs, Harpies, etc – who all then feature in the historical stories of those times.

The Magi of the Healing Temples became above their station and stepped into Ego, demanding that they had better and separate living quarters and should be revered because of their growing status.

The downfall of Atlantis came because of the inter-breeding of the species and the ego, and therefore the experiment failed. Some fled to Egypt to create a new world there, whilst others returned to their places of origin.

The island of Atlantis was then flooded and sunk to remove the disharmony that it had created.

How were the pyramids made?

The civilisation which fled from Atlantis to ancient Egypt became the much revered Pharaohs.

They lived among the humans, who created pyramids as temples and as a way of preserving their dead. The pyramids were built by humans using levitation tools and equipment from the spirit beings.

When a Pharaoh died, the humans believed that they would be reincarnated. Each Pharaoh was buried carefully in a sarcophagus and surrounded by their worldly fortune, in preparation for their reincarnation. However, the spiritual beings did not return after their deaths.

Why was Stonehenge built and why were stone circles positioned as they were?

The interstellar beings built various structures to harness natural energy centres around the world – Stonehenge in the UK being the primary one of them.

Stonehenge lies on a line of energy which is part of a grid network, called ley lines. The ancient ones used stone as a marker to perform ceremonies and connect with the energies which were inherent in that site, and which would increase the potency of that ceremony. For example, couples could make love there, druids could perform their ceremonies, using it as a ritualistic site for sacrifice (and then taken to a burial ground).

Stone circles have been found around the world, which we believe were created on those pieces of land because of their position on the ley line grid. They have been found to connect in with many calendar events and sacred geometry.

They have always been gathering places, sites for celebration with attendees perhaps holding hands in a circle around the stones.

Each stone at a stone circle has a different vibration – it is common that people who feel an affinity with Stonehenge in particular do not feel the same affinity with a similar site at Avebury – and vice versa. The stones in each circle are positioned astrologically and retain something of the events which occurred there.

Sacred geometry comes into play here around the arrangement of the stones themselves, in circles, in groups, and as doorways.

Stonehenge now

Stonehenge as it was

Each of the stones in Stonehenge were originally joined in a circle, with five individual large doorways in the centre. We believe it was a sacred site containing a group of portals, an inter-galactic doorway through which one could travel to and from other planets and star systems, as well as around the Earth itself.

These portals were used as a doorway to the living library of Gaia, by High Council beings coming together from multi-dimensions, along with human representatives from the different continents of the world.

After its original use came to an end, other civilisations have used and abused the stone circles around the world.

Stonehenge became more of a sacrificial site for births, marriages and deaths.

How were the stone circles built? It is believed that the stones came from Wales – so how would they have been moved from there to Stonehenge and Avebury? These stone circles – and other ancient phenomenon – were created centuries ago, without modern machinery and without modern technology.

Those who created the stone circles knew how to use their powers to levitate and move stones in order to make other structures like the ancient pyramids – we believe this is what happened at Stonehenge. Or did it? If they used the site as a portal for transportation, why not transport the stones there in a similar way and use the portal doorways to move the stones from Wales?

Crop circles and other phenomena

Sacred geometry can be found in all of nature – spirals, pentagons, cubes, pyramids, etc. The shape and structure in which something is formed can determine an object's vibration – and can be related to the chakra system, by relating each chakra with a different shape. Our perception is that a crop circle is created by a vibration from outside our atmosphere.

We know from elsewhere in this book that sound and vibration have effects on things around us. Our vibrations as humans can have some effect on the elements around us – perhaps linking with weather systems to cause the crop circles to be made by the wind.

Crop circles could also be a calling card from another race – but whoever or whatever created them, we should take note that our response to them opens us up to possibilities in the future and beyond.

Walking trails in south America can be seen to trace out patterns in the desert – but only when viewed from above. How were these walking trails created? Who or what guided the front walker in each case to mark out the trail?

No airplanes were available, for example, when creating the lines – which can only be viewed in totality from the air via airplane or drones.

We believe they were guided by inspiration or thought – or gave themselves up to guidance from a spiritual being who wanted to create a visual representation of living creatures. Perhaps the lead walker was on a shamanic trail, or it was a group of shamans, walking through the desert, walking the path of an animal or creature to gain the powers of that animal.

What is the truth behind the myth of Jesus and Mary Magdalene's relationship?

Jesus was a man, and was also a teacher and leader for souls that needed direction. He was known as a spiritual communicator – he conversed with God and other spirits as well. Before he was born, it was foretold that he was coming – Archangel Gabriel said that this "King of Men" would be coming forward.

To pay homage to this new-born it was told that three men travelled to meet the new King – Casper, Balthazar and Melchior. In other lifetimes, these three men have had other lives and are now known as Ascended Masters in their own right.

During Jesus' childhood, he was in a family unit where the father was a carpenter. Another family member was known as John the Baptist – this led to the spiritual teachings that Jesus had from being very little.

Mary Magdalene was a spiritual initiate of the ancient goddess Isis. There is a school of thought that Mary Magdalene was a High Priestess, who was trained to help Jesus when she met him. Others say that Mary Magdalene had been Isis herself in a previous life. A further thought is that Mary Magdalene was a Higher Being in her own right. This may explain why she held equal standing within the group of disciples, which would have been unheard of at the time for a woman amongst a group of men.

Jesus communicated with the Highest Beings – some say he was a prophet, a teacher, a healer and helped people, and married Mary Magdalene and they had a lineage – he was executed on the cross because he didn't conform. Some believe he wasn't executed and they left together and that their lineage continues today and their DNA is still active. Others say Mary was his whore, woman, slave.

We believe that Jesus was an empowered man, kind, caring and thoughtful of others' needs. He was also nomadic and therefore ego was not attached to him. He would have helped people and they would have returned that help via food, water and a bed for the night. He also spoke as an ambassador promoting a spiritual way of life, understanding the humble origins of his birth and the terrain that he walked. He wasn't a rich man, but he shared whatever he did acquire with others.

We believe he took Mary Magdalene as his wife and they shared a life together, and along that path others of the twelve disciples joined them to talk about their teachings, so that they could go out into the world and spread the word of God.

"Power" then was regarded as possessions and wealth, birth right and authority. Jesus's power was his voice, which was against the ruling authority's beliefs and control. He was an activist for peace, not power.

We believe they had children – a girl – before Jesus was executed. The girl then went onto continue the teachings of the initiates. Her lineage was kept a secret from those in power because they would probably have killed her.

Jesus in his own right, his Higher self is known as Sanander. He channelled the healing abilities in order to help people – he was a walking, breathing, healing source of therapy. In the spirit world, where he now resides, he is a teacher and guide of healing modalities.

Some believe that we are all children of God, the one source. Other people believe that he is the Christed one.

Did the dinosaurs really become extinct because of a meteor or was there really a meteor?

Prehistoric life

Planet Earth is a planet of experimentation and exploration for various extra-terrestrial species. The Earth herself is perhaps one of only a handful of such planets that has been created to harbour such a wide variety of life forms. It could be said that the Earth is part of a big game, a huge game of chess with multiple colours and multiple strategies. A place where ET beings are free to experiment with the DNA found here and produce myriad possibilities of life.

No one person can say for sure the real reasons for the creation and population of the dinosaurs but it is our feeling that extra-terrestrials seeded the earth with primitive animals, such as the dinosaurs to explore life and watch it thrive and evolve in their environments, themselves created. (The whole premise of Jurassic park is closer to the truth than many would realise).

We know from science that Earth looked very different from how it does today. There were fewer continents and the weather conditions were much different. It is suggested that these prehistoric life forms thrived on Earth for millions of years then were suddenly wiped out by a large meteor that struck the earth.

This meteor struck the Earth and irrevocably altered the planet and landscape for good. This event in one way or another could be a form of terra-forming, a method of preparing the ground for a new life to evolve.

The group of extra-terrestrials responsible for life forms at that time decided it was time to change the game and began to experiment with early hominids. The arrival of the homo sapiens allowed more advanced consciousness (souls) to incarnate and our present evolution was born from this.

The early Neanderthals were primitive, cave dwelling beings but through spiritual intervention evolved and formed simple communities. They honoured the land and animals and gave thanks to the Earth for food. They honoured the dead and these simple communities changed through migration and environmental input resulting in the different races we see today.

So it is we see that the extra-terrestrials would intervene and develop the brain capacity and other DNA modifications to the early hominids resulting in our present day homo sapiens.

Did they do this to allow more advanced consciousness to incarnate or was they another objective? The landscape changed and as mentioned the landmass of the Earth changed resulting in seven continents.

It should be mentioned that Gaia, earths consciousness has had a huge say in what evolves and thrives upon her lush land. She periodically re-establishes balance to enable different life forms to mature upon her.

Developing civilisations

Throughout history we are now aware of numerous civilisations that have thrived upon the earth, some more successful than others.

It is interesting to note that we currently have seven continents, do they have a connection with the seven chakras of the human body and perhaps with Gaia herself?

They may do, but we know that each civilisation recognised a god or gods and worshipped them in numerous ways.

This common thread of god worship suggests that man has always remembered his spiritual routes, even if his rational mind has forgotten this truth.

Another interesting civilisation that has been suggested to exist is that of inner earth dwellers. A race of beings with their own light, water and energy supply. These beings could have been part of the collective of ET beings responsible for keeping an eye on the developing human race.

The biggest question: who am I?

Human self:

We are complex biological forms a vehicle to house an aspect of your high self. The body needs certain things to be able to function and to grow – when we come into this world we are then catapulted in to the family aspect, develop an ego, develop a sense of separation.

There are many reasons why we come onto the planet. Some people come as workers, the 'drones', as they are sustaining everyone else – and then you have those that are the 'queen bee' in an authoritative role.

But whichever role you take, you are here for a purpose and no one is better than anyone else or should feel that they are better than anyone else. We are here for ourselves. Your journey is yours alone – what you are here to learn is your own life mission. You are allowed to be selfish and selfless whilst you are visiting this earth.

Spiritual self:

The spiritual being is far more vast than our human minds can imagine. It is on a journey of experience and exploration.

Every spiritual being is different and interacts differently on the vast spiritual planes of existence – each soul will experience them differently. Each spiritual being that comes to reside in an earth body will learn something vital to its role system in the spiritual world.

For example: someone who works tirelessly helping others through charity and selfless devotion to others is then not thinking about themselves – they are not looking at themselves as charitable. Always giving and not getting anything back is not an exchange of energy, it's a one-way street.

Whereas someone who gives to others may also keep something back for themselves, and is living in duality because they are both self and self-less.

Consider the tree of life: (for this example, we are using an oak tree)

The root system represents the many lives that the Monad inhabits, each one learning and growing and filtering its knowledge acquired into the Monad in order to grow and flourish and spread its beautiful branches above. As above so below.

What is the purpose of the human life?

Everyone's spiritual purpose is different – think how many things we have already looked at, think how difficult relationships can be. Think about forgiving and moving on. How does it sit with you to be open and honest all the time in your relationships? Does it benefit you to do so? If you are asked "does my bum look big in this?" is it better to reply "I've seen you in something better" rather than a straight out "yes"?

It comes down to – do you want to be happy or unhappy, and what lessons do you look to learn while you are here? What can you distance yourself from within your life, in order to measure your level of happiness in the big scheme of things. This is in contrast to feeling lost within everything, the unhappy victim, the deflated balloon, unhappy with life.

At what point do you decide what's good in your life and what isn't, and what's your purpose?

For most souls it is about self-realisation and self-recreation. We are all trying to realise who we are in our lives – but there is more to it than that. There are those in the world who kill and murder, and who teach a lesson through their horrible acts. Your spiritual being may have chosen to come to earth to be the villain, or to be the damsel in distress. We take from life what we need.

A series of events will happen in the world and we take from it what our soul needs. If you empathise and then want to be an activist after an incident, you can do this. But there has to be a villain somewhere along the line for us to learn from.

As our spiritual being comes to join our human form at birth, the choices have already been made for what path we tread. Our purpose spiritually is to decide how we are best going to travel that path, what we are going to learn from it, how we choose to deal with the hand that we are dealt, from a human perspective.

The spiritual being jumps into the human body at any point during pregnancy or birth – and learns from each human life that it inhabits.

We can spend our lives wondering "why and when did I sign up for my life to feel so hard?" – or we can choose to look at the experiences we have and how we have grown from having them. This is what our spiritual being is doing – learning from the various elements of human experience, before moving on to inhabiting another human body.

We have to come to our own answers about all of the questions we come across in our lives – how we live with our decisions is by understanding why we made those decisions. Looking backwards helps us to understand how to move forward.

Everything we do feeds into who and what we are – and into the next human body that our spirit will inhabit.

To enable oneself to truly understand the soul's purpose is to sit quietly in a safe and free space, allowing the busy thoughts to gradually dissipate into a mindless silence.

Questioning the mind can take practice and even the most regular meditators can experience the odd unwanted thought.

How do you feel being quiet? Just being able to be at peace with yourself, away from drama – that of your own or others? It is inviting a silent retreat into your own state of being.

You are in contact with your true soul being at all times. It's just that we have at times selective hearing as in we choose when we wish to connect with our high source.

To understand your purpose is to allow your high conscious to come forward to blend in the present. Ask yourself for a clear direction and allow your pathway to unfold.

Upon the earth, everyone's soul purpose is diverse and different from another.

When entering this world we come with a clean sheet, a blank canvas of learning.

From birth we are conditioned by our peers. This is where your personality begins to emerge. The strongest will accomplish their mission tasks at an early age. It is an endless study to fulfil your plan.

Imagine a ladder and each rung is another goal attained. Some ladders are small and only have a few rungs, these rungs may have a vast space between them, hence the lesson could be arduous. For others, there are many rungs and with little gaps.

Going back to meditation techniques: it is always good to look into the different ways to meditate as one might help you more than another to connect.

Please use this space to record your responses to any questions which are either posed in this chapter or which arise from it.

Questions:

How did this chapter make you feel?

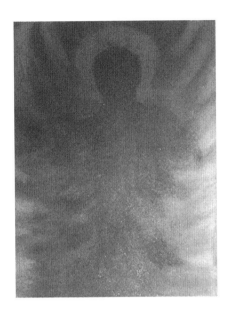

Ring the bell to sound your arrival.

Announce to the world that you are here.

Stand up straight, arms to the side —

Smile greatly and light up the sky.

15. Success and achievement

This is a chapter of thought-provoking questions. We asked ourselves, whether we should answer them for you – but decided it is best for each individual reader to find their own answers, as they appear to you.

We cannot answer your questions for you but we instead welcome you to look at your own perceptions and note your own answers to the following questions on how you measure and gauge success and achievement.

Is success having vision…. somebody's vision of their future? Or is it imagination?

Are you a visionary or do you just have a great imagination?

How do you see yourself and are you achieving what you have envisaged you would like to be? Are you more than that?

Have you superseded your quest for self?

Have you made the decision of what you want to be? Have you defined yourself by someone else's success?

Is success dependent on others?

On the question of what do we want to be, who are we to decide? And who are we to decide what success is?

Do you measure success by money or deeds?

Is success measured by the amount of money you have in your bank, or the level of inner peace you feel about the way you have conducted your life, and how you have done this, and how you are deemed by other people for your kindness and actions, not for what you can buy them?

Are people happy to be in your presence, just for you?

Is success measured then by just being you and do you make a difference?

How can you make a difference?

To make a difference in your life or someone else's, the key is to know who you are and what part you play in someone's life experience, and what part you allow others to play in your life because this is your own success story.

The word "success" originates from Latin regarding "what comes close after" an accomplishment.

Success is often measured by quantity, not quality – how many seats sold, how much money made, how many books sold, etc. If a job is worth doing, is it still worth doing well and to your highest standards? Everyone holds different standards and has different expectations of themselves.

Exercise

How do you measure success? What characteristics, mannerisms, behaviours, actions and abilities do you think that a successful person has? And how would you measure the opposite of success?

Use the following 2 pages to create your list / diagram / image of a successful person and an unsuccessful person.

Your image of a successful person

Your image of an unsuccessful person

Our imagining of a successful person is:

And our imagining of an unsuccessful person is:

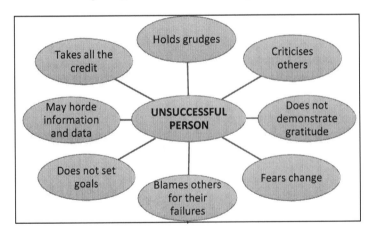

Please use this space to record your responses to any questions which are either posed in this chapter or which arise from it.

Questions:

How did this chapter make you feel?

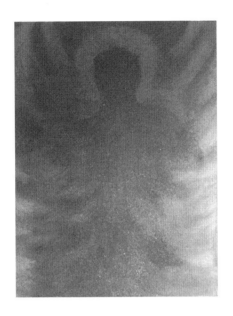

Build your wall of protection.

Keep it strong as it holds something special

— your soul

16. Depression and Oppression

Depression and oppression of your soul could manifest, because you are not fulfilling your soul's Earth mission.

This relates to depression as a spiritual being, and then the oppression within that realm – rather than depression in general human life.

A depression is a spiritual wake-up call, a soul calling, you have not listened to what is going on in your life, your body is going through a series of conditions that you have not listened to, and the soul cries out for this – leading to depression, and this can lead to extremes like suicide.

How does one avoid depression? If we find ourselves becoming depressed, how do we get out of that? What are the signs and how do we seek the right help, rather than going down the route of medicine and drugs which just suppress the soul's desire to become more involved in the human body. Maybe depression is a suppression of the soul – the ego is running out, being a dual player in the person, and the sense of separation and fear becomes so strong that the person wilts inside and could turn to drugs in order to cope.

It is really difficult to be spiritual in the human. This goes back to the book title – about how to be human when you are spirit. If you're not here doing what you are meant to be doing, that's the soul being oppressed – which moves us into being a spiritual being.

With Annette's work as a medium and a holistic therapist, the various clients that come to see her have a common denominator of relationships, and how difficult it is to be in and remain in a relationship – whether that be parental, romantic, work-related or general friendships. This means opening and sharing your life with those said relationships, to the point of asking "is the relationship worth you losing your own precious time?" You don't get wasted time back. If you are not authentic within yourself, afraid to be yourself in a relationship, for fears of not being liked, you will never be in a true relationship with anybody, due to the fear of rejection. It is imperative to be authentic and truthful and committing yourself fully to every relationship, not going half measures on anything.

The one person you will hurt by going half measures is yourself. When we arrive on the planet and are birthed, we are here to progress our own soul and also to aid in the progress other beings' development. We are, in effect, part of Gaia's work – Earth's involvement in our soul's evolution.

You enter the planet with a birth certificate and exit via a death certificate. In between you have a piece of paper to say you are married – and another to say you are divorced. A P45 to have left a job, and a P60 to declare yearly earnings. There are also driving licences, qualification certificates etc. They are all proof of life. They are a record of your existence in this life.

Within past life and future life, you are part of the Akashic records. Those pieces of paper can't help the heart – they are just legal documents. When you have scars on the heart from a particular relationship, mending those scars and having the tools to do so, that's the human conditioning. Some would say "pick yourself up, start again, plenty of fish in the sea, always another job out there, they weren't good enough for you" – these are common ways that people would give you a pat on the back to say "everything's OK" but the point is that you have to sew yourself together and reconcile what's happened. It may take a long time to do that – it might even take a few relationships to understand what went wrong in the first one – what drew you to them, what energy was there, did you choose them by default because no one else was available? Look at the lessons you learned within that relationship or within a job role. It takes effort to look at yourself and see the mirror within. This is the reason for writing this book – to look at our relationships and how they mould our future, so that we hopefully don't have to return in another life to repeat the patterns, that we have not managed to learn in this one.

Experiences of past lives have shown that we literally come back to work on and through past karma – do unto others as you want to be treated yourself – which is personal responsibility.

You don't get a certificate for being yourself – we get them in our society for the purposes of measuring what we have done. This doesn't happen in other tribal societies – the Shaman doesn't have a certificate. They may have marks to honour the coming of age, or a ceremony or ritual. The Western society depicts the certificate as measure of standing in the community – this fits under logic, control and proof of life.

A prophet doesn't have a certificate for being a prophet, and to be a spiritual being, no certificate is required. Reputation is their proof. The wisdom and knowledge that they have acquired is their 'dissertation of life'.

Please use this space to record your responses to any questions which are either posed in this chapter or which arise from it.

Questions:

How did this chapter make you feel?

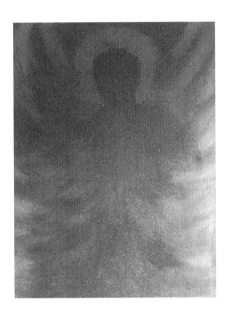

A little light glimpse into who you are:

shining and beautiful

17. Personal responsibility: Mental health and autism

This is such a hefty subject.

For this chapter, we thought long and hard about how to talk about it. Because of the work we do as therapists and mediums, we do come across a wide range of the general public who are suffering, or know someone who suffers with, a condition under the banner of mental health. Therefore we felt we should do an overview of the subject.

Please note that neither of us is medically trained and therefore not qualified to offer medical advice. We have however both had experience of working with people within the mental health spectrum, Mark as teacher in Special Needs, and Annette as a medium and complementary health therapist.

If you are suffering from a mental health problem or know someone else who is, please seek advice from your general practitioner or care provider – and if you are not happy then or would rather choose a different route, please seek alternative methods from complementary health.

There are a lot of organisations and groups that are there to help and offer advice for anyone suffering from mental health problems – please do not suffer in silence when your world may already be full of silence. You may feel alone in a world full of people but please know that there is always somebody there to offer a helping hand if you look for it.

We want to apologise that we can't touch upon everything under the mental health banner in this one chapter – that would be a whole book in itself. For this exercise, we are talking about the spiritual self and mental health – and whatever impacts these have.

A person suffering from mental health issues is a victim of some sort – some people don't know they even have an issue, others feel it very acutely.

How is it that, in the last decade, mental health seems to be the answer or reason for so many problems worldwide?

Depression: mental health.

Autism: mental health.

Statistically there is a steady decline in general wellbeing. What influences this?

Mental health has become more prominent in this decline – and just about every other person that you come across has experienced some issue relating to mental health to some degree.

Where is this coming from?

As a spiritual being, you do not have mental health problems – but when you come in to the human world you come up across those problems, so is it DNA or the body or does spirit not sit well in the body? External factors also come into play – diets can change how we live, environmental issues like pollution play their part, plus we have societal pressure with media telling us what to buy, what to look like, what to do. There are lots of external negative pressures on us. People associate more with their physical body than with their spiritual body. We experience fear more, fear of sickness and disease and what it can do to the body – bringing dis-ease.

The more that the external pressures tell us we must be perfect, the harder and more impossible it becomes.

But if you do not subscribe to the societal views of glitz and glamour, why might you then suffer from mental health problems? Is it because you are ostracising yourself from that world?

If you say you are not worried about what other people think of you, why might you suffer a mental health problem? Is saying this in itself a fallacy, an untruth? Do we all care in some small way what others think about us?

If you are living a vegan life, making sure you only eat healthy foods – and you live in an area away from pollution and away from society – but still suffer from depression, what causes this?

Could it be as simple as you don't want to be here, you are rejecting being in your body, and your body is rejecting you?

Mental health issues can arise from trouble during the birthing process – a baby starved of oxygen in the birth canal, for example. Or a trauma in later life – both of which causes physical trauma to the brain.

What we are going to talk about next could be seen as divisive.

We want people to think about where they are in their life, and to be aware that there are bigger things going on outside of yourself.

As a spirit being, learning and developing the soul can only be achieved whilst it is in a learning process. Coming here on the earth into an inhibiting body and mind can, for that spirit, be very restrictive, especially being in the human body when the spirit is so vast. Choosing the life we live, whether it be of sound body and mind or having a physical or learning difficulty under the banner of mental health constricts the soul whilst you are in the human body.

The spirit chooses the life that it wants to live and experience. It is imperative that we expand our awareness and learn.

Please note that it is the *spirit* that has chosen the life that it wants to live – not the human it inhabits. And it is the human that has to live the life, with the spirit inside them.

Therefore you could find yourself in conflict with your own spirit, arguing "why did you allow this to happen, to put me in this state where I am not able to function as a human being, and not able to enjoy the earth plane to its full potential?"

To which the spirit will answer that having a body that restricts you has shown you what it is like, and how you deal with that – and it is also learning for the people around you. You may have chosen this life for yourself not for you, but as spirit you chose it to help another person to learn what it is like to care for that person – because we are all one.

A child that has been starved of oxygen at birth may have developmental problems – mental or physical. Their soul may be only partially present and not able to communicate – but the adult helps the child into adulthood, helping the child to understand what it is like to have another individual love them unconditionally. Each action causes a reaction in someone else.

As a loved one, you may not want the responsibility of caring for a mentally ill family member or friend. This is where the healers of the world can help to talk off some of the pressure, to help them to function in a more 'normal' way.

As a medium, it has been an honour and a privilege to communicate with children and adults alike who have no physical voice and cannot communicate with their loved ones for themselves. I have worked with these people and spoken with their spirits so that they can pass their message to their loved ones. This can in many cases have been the first real communication that they have had in their lifetimes with their loved ones.

This also can be said for those that are suffering with Dementia and Alzheimer's, because you are talking to the soul of that being, without the human mind interrupting. Coma patients can also be reached. This is why being a medium comes with such responsibility – and a huge one at that – but it is also so profound that you are able to touch someone in such a way that conveys just the smallest – or the hugest – of words (the most powerful of which are "I love you") to their loved ones.

Only when you are spiritually aware that your spirit chose the life that you live, then can you question "why did my spirit choose this life, as it is really hard?"

Please use this space to record your responses to any questions which are either posed in this chapter or which arise from it.

Questions:

How did this chapter make you feel?

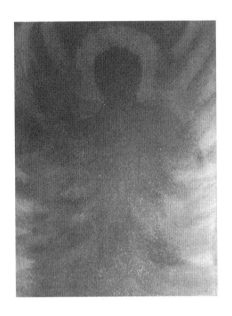

To kiss your frog is to know yourself

for we all metamorphose

when we leave the safety of our lily pad.

18. Music, dance and sound to soothe the soul and lift your energy vibrations

Sound is part of our lives – everything makes a sound. The first sound we hear is our mother's heartbeat – and the first thing a mother hears from their baby is its screams. Our last heartbeat and our last breathe will be our last sounds, barring the internal gurgles after the soul has left the body and the body starts to decay.

Sound is vibration – we are all vibrating beings, that's why sound has such a big effect on our bodies, minds and souls. Everything has a vibration and a sound – the earth, animals, objects – we are constantly surrounded by sound. Sounds play a big part in our health, relationships to ourselves and to others.

How we use our voice is important: do we speak with authority and assertiveness? Or do you feel you do not have a voice? If you are born with a working voice box then you have the opportunity to use it for communication – and do you use it in a positive or negative way, to help or to hinder?

If you lose your voice, are you losing it knowingly or are you letting someone else speak for you? Your voice changes over time – choirboys lose the ability to reach the high notes as they hit puberty, and older people lose their singing tone and control as the voice box and larynx ages. Illnesses – tonsillitis, laryngitis, through to cancer – all can affect the voice.

The throat is connected to the throat chakra system which helps a person to express their individuality, their inner truth, to speak their truth, to communicate. There can be disfunctions in the throat chakra and it's not always from this lifetime – there could have been a throat-related injury in a past life, for example someone who feels that their voice is strangled in this life may have suffered from something throat-related in a past life.

Everybody has a different musical taste – from the sounds that we dance to in celebration of life and the first dance at a wedding or prom, music can also be our exit songs at our funeral. The choice of words or tunes can play a huge part in saying "goodbye". Have you noticed how many people choose "My Way" for a funeral, and watch the "final curtain" close around their loved one's coffin at the crematorium? Certain songs can be very popular.

Sound and music and movement have been important for centuries – Masii warriors have been jumping and dancing throughout their history. And now music and sound play a huge part in our entertainment, in terms of music accompanying films or TV shows, background sounds throughout, advertising jingles, etc. Does the film make the song famous or does the song make the film more memorable – look back to the advent of films: the original films were silent and in black and white, with a piano player in the auditorium. The first "talkie" movie was "The Jazz Singer". Would "The Lion King" be as popular without "The Circle of Life" or would "Frozen" be as well-known without "Let It Go?"

There are sounds that can grate on some people – the fingernail down a blackboard, the sounds of a Formula

One race, a baby screaming, a mosquito flying round your bedroom late at night.

Yet there are sounds which can fill us with wonder – the sound of the waves, the roar of a tiger, the constant noise of nature in a forest.

Some sounds do not resonate with everyone – it's finding your own harmonic resonance that is important. Equally, if you find a sound that grates on you, work through it, it may be something that you can work on until you can tolerate it. You might go for a gong bath, for example – and you may be one of those people who can find them very soothing, yet there are other people who might find it unbearable. More of this shortly…

Your harmony may be very different from someone else's.

Astrologically, every planet and star has a vibration – and as everything is moving, they all have an effect on each other. The tiniest movement can affect everything, just as the largest movement can.

Sound and music have been researched scientifically, two areas of interest are:

Dr Masuro Emoto (Japanese author, researcher, photographer and entrepreneur) claimed that human consciousness has an effect on the molecular structure of water. Emoto's conjecture evolved over the years, and his early work explored his belief that water could react to positive thoughts and words, and that polluted water could be cleaned through prayer and positive visualization. He projected sound at bowls of water and found that it produced geometric patterns in the water.

Hans Jenny (Swiss physician and natural scientist) coined the term cymatics to describe acoustic effects of sound wave phenomena. He projected sound onto plates, and found that this made interesting patterns, depending on the type of music – conjecturing that hard rock music can be quite disturbing for some people, whilst classical music / pure tones is very relaxing and can be seen to promote harmony within the body.

This is not to say that any type of music is "good" or "bad" – we can all enjoy different types of music at different times, and sometimes a bit of heavy rock can be very appropriate whilst a quieter more sombre tune would not be suitable to an event. You may prefer to jog whilst listening to a pounding beat, a motivational talker, a playlist of sad songs after a breakup, through to a positive playlist to bring about a happier mood.

Whatever your choice, go with whatever makes your soul sing and your body move – this can promote wellbeing and balance. Our very vocabulary includes the expression "being of sound mind" – indicating whether somebody is well-balanced.

An exercise to undertake with your partner is to write a list of ten songs (which you may choose to record onto a CD) that you feel is related to your relationship with them, what they mean to you. Ask your partner to do the same exercise about you – and see if you have both matched any particular songs.

Every sound has a rhythm and structure – rhythm is a strong, regular repeated pattern of movement or sound. The first sound we hear, we have already stated, is our mother's heartbeat – along with the sounds of our family – from when we are in the womb. Our brains have a natural frequency and rhythm, and can be influenced externally. So, for example, if we hear a repetitive drumbeat, it can alter our brainwaves into different states of consciousness.

We have different levels of consciousness within the brain (alpha, beta, gamma, delta waves etc), each of which can be influenced through differing speeds of beats. As with the musicality of a sound, the rhythm of the sound can bring us to a more relaxed or more agitated state. Our heart has similar resonance to a pendulum in a clock, reacting to other frequencies around it.

The therapy of sound

Sound has many therapeutic qualities.

Sound therapists state that our bodies are made up of "energy frequencies" and certain sonic frequencies can be used to reattune our energy frequencies if they go "off key". The role of the sound therapist is to promote wellbeing in the body through the use of direct sound. A multitude of instruments can be used, such as gongs, frame drums and Himalayan singing bowls, as well as voice, tuning forks or recorded music. Musical instruments like bells, harp, xylophone, triangle can also be used.

Drumming can be very therapeutic, promoting vibrational change. Adults can find this useful in a group situation, whilst children may find it therapeutic to bang a wooden spoon on a saucepan lid.

A sound therapy session could include: an individual or group of individuals in a room, finding a comfortable place either lying or sitting or down. They then relax and listen to the sound therapist's voice, talking them through the process and relaxing them with meditative techniques, and then moving onto using the instrument(s). The length of therapy session can vary from half an hour to a few hours – some gong baths, for example, can last all night or all day for a workshop – as long as it is needed. After the sound therapy is concluded, attendees may have experienced a wide variety of reactions, which might include falling asleep, a change in thinking, anxiety, visualisations, clarity of mind, agitation, decision making, invigoration.

As you see, the effects of a sound therapy treatment can be powerful, in fact life-changing. This further supports the scientific evidence that sound can be transformational.

The effects of sound throughout our day

We live our lives by sounds, and can often make approximations of "telling the time" from them. Certain sounds can be predicable at certain times – we know that the cockerel will crow each morning, and the birds will "tweet" their dawn chorus welcoming the sun back, whilst owls hoot throughout a night of darkness. A clock will tick and tock throughout the day, and bells may sound every quarter hour – plus we set an alarm on our clock to wake us each morning.

A piece of music is made of different sounds. When combined together, this music can send us to tears, send us to sleep, wake us up, make us dance.

This need not be formalised "music" – there is musicality to be found in the leaves and the trees, in the sounds of animals, in whale noise (often referred to as "whale music" due to the tones), in birdsong. Many people use musical sounds, like frog noises, rainforest sound or whale music to aid them in going to sleep at night, using phone apps or pre-recorded CDs.

Please use this space to record your responses to any questions which are either posed in this chapter or which arise from it.

Questions:

How did this chapter make you feel?

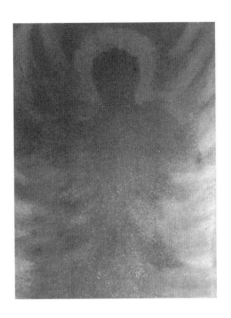

Life is so very precious...

Enjoy being present and

spending time with the ones that you love

19.   Travel- the journey of your life

Mortality – and Morgue-ality

Have you got a burning urge to do something before you die? Or are you at peace with the idea of dying and know that if you died tonight in your sleep you are where you want to be, with the partner that you wanted to be with?

If you knew when you are going to die – how much of our life would you want to rewind in order to clear the cobwebs of your life?

If you knew how long you had left in this life, would you make a conscious choice to do things differently in the time you have left? Would you do charitable work, volunteering, or carry on in your job?

How many people have asked "what is the meaning of life?" It's anything you want it to be.

Are you happy with your life – and if you are not, then surely that should be your biggest question!

Death and Dying – dispelling the myths

Death and dying can be looked at in a positive way, especially when considering our place and role in this world.

Leaving our earthly body – and dying in this life – doesn't mean you are dying from your life as a spiritual being.

Thinking about your point of passing could promote more questions: for example, do you know that you are about to pass, and if you knew, who would you like to have with you, and where would you like it to be, if you had a choice?

Would you like to be in bed, cuddled up – or sat on a park bench in a favourite park with partner at your side, and a big phone call with lots of friends and family telling you it's OK to go now? Or would you like to be – possibly with your partner – in nature somewhere, perhaps by the sea or in a wooded forest? Or would you like to be completely on your own in silence somewhere?

It's only our attachment to this life that holds us to it – we need to each accept that we are in one life of many. The mind wants to reject the notion of finality.

Soul midwifery is deemed to be relatively new – a lot of mediums, healers, nurses, doctors and hospice care are already helping the soul to pass over with the work that they do.

The continued love and support that they give for this each and every day, is a job that they have chosen to do.

Helping the soul to move on

There are many questions around the point of death.

Has the person achieved what they want to achieve? Will their family be there waiting for them? Will they pass happily?

Annette recalls as a healer she gave soul healing to a gentleman, telling him he was surrounded by angels – and he said he knew that they were there, and he wasn't afraid of dying as he felt their presence.

As a human being, when we pass away, doctors, ministers, funeral directors all have to take their part but at the end of the day it is the person that is left to make the arrangements who is there to grieve and hand over their loved one to a complete stranger to clean and care for them and help them move on to the next stage.

This is generally done with great care and attention to detail. For many of us, we have no idea how to organise a funeral until we have to do it.

The funeral process

Many people have no idea of what the funeral process is, until they come to the point of having to arrange a funeral.

After death, funeral directors are given the go ahead to proceed – which will involve collecting the deceased and take them to the morgue / mortuary, to await further instructions either from the general practitioner or from the coroner.

The family, friend or whoever will make the arrangements will then sit down with the funeral arranger to go through the procedure in fine detail, whilst filling in paperwork.

Should the family wish to pay their respects in the chapel of rest, the funeral director will then wash and dress the deceased in a respectful way.

The grieving partner then chooses where their loved ones' remains are then placed, through cremation or burial – or natural burial (buried usually in a wooded area with no marker for the grave, and in a biodegradable casket). A traditional burial would have a marker – for example, a headstone – and burial of cremated remains normally is marked with a name plaque. Alternatively, the family can hold onto the remains to scatter – but permission is required from the appropriate authorities.

Otherwise, the body can be sent direct to the crematorium in a standard coffin, without going through the funeral home preparations. In these instances, there is usually no family present at the crematorium, and a memorial service can be held at some other time afterwards as a celebratory get together of the person's life.

You may choose to bury your loved ones' cremated ashes or have a full burial in your garden, but be aware that you may have to change the deeds for the house to that of a cemetery.

More than one burial in a piece of land currently carries with it a legal requirement to list that piece of land as a cemetery So a farmer, for example, who allows more than one burial on their land must change the deeds to list the farm as a cemetery, and a permit is required.

Planning and arranging your own funeral

The other part to death is that you can plan your own funeral in advance. The cost of funerals increases every year – but if you choose to pay for your funeral in advance, this doesn't mean you can't change your stipulations along the way. Many institutions offer funeral plans that you can pay in instalments. This allows you to pay for the funeral that you ask for and also ensures that your family cannot then change your plans, so your funeral will go ahead as you wish it to be. Equally, it also removes the pressure from the family in having to make the decisions on what to do during their grieving time.

Should you look into this further please search online for more information.

Human life end – spiritual continuance

At the point of human death, as a spiritual being, the spirit leaves the body at the point of passing.

It is perceived in some religious sectors that the "etheric chord" is still attached at death and does not detach for three days, therefore surmising that the spirit stays with the body until the third day.

It is the thought of some that this is depictive of Jesus at his death and crucifixion, that he died and his spirit stayed with his body for three days.

As spiritual mediums, we do not necessarily agree with this three day process – we have seen some spirits stay with their bodies after death, but very few in comparison with who leave at the point death.

Consider for yourself – when you pass, would you prefer that your spirit stays with your body for three days, watching nature take its course?

Or would you prefer to stay with your family to assist them in their grieving process?

Or would you prefer to move on to another plane to heal your spirit and then return? Many deceased spirits are in fact present at their own funerals – is this a form of "morbid curiosity"?

The dying process

When your higher spirit speaks to your body's inner spirit and says it is time for you to pass, then in some way your body will start to reject your spirit aspect, and therefore causing illness to the body.

Is this reversible? And can you choose to stay?

Anyone with a terminal illness, who may be going through many forms of radical treatment, could be hoping for some sort of intervention – whether medical, divine or otherwise.

Could this purely be a wakeup call?

Is this a call for us to change our life patterns, our self-destructive processes, change how we eat, what we eat, reduce our stress levels, etc?

Or could it that within our human conditioning the instinctual fight for survival is what drives us?

Is it in our conditioning to fight, and is it our fear of death that makes us want to stay here?

What is the learning that we might gain in the next life as a result of demanding / fighting / choosing to stay on longer in this one?

Eventually it will be your higher spirit that makes this decision. Not forgetting the added complication that the decision was actually already made before birth before our spirit entered this body! Everyone's timeline is individual, everyone's story is already written.

Annette says if you can, enjoy the life that you live – because you will always then be able to look back and say "do you know what? I lived that life to the best of my potential."

Please use this space to record your responses to any questions which are either posed in this chapter or which arise from it.

Questions:

How did this chapter make you feel?

THE END

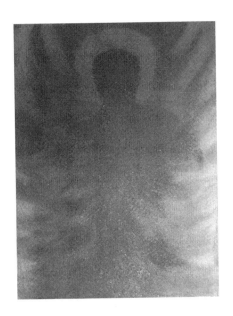

*To kindred spirits, who love
unconditionally.*

*When you finally say goodbye, what you
are left with, are the memories....*

*Hold them within your heart and
remember the love....*

Your place in time, just not the right time

xxx

Glossary of terms used in this book

For the purposes of this book, our definitions of the following terms are:

- **Akashic Records**

  Akasha is the Sanskrit word for "aether" or "atmosphere" is a record of all thoughts, emotions, actions and events that have occurred.

  It is believed to be etheric in nature.

- **Ascended Master**

  An Ascended Master is a being believed to be a spiritually enlightened human who has completed earthly incarnations and now offers assistance/ guidance to human and spirit beings alike.

- **Chakra**

  from Sanskrit cakra 'wheel or circle' the body contains chakras which are known as energy centres.

- **Crystal / indigo / rainbow children**

  These are children who are part of the spiritual community and have come here with the gifts of being highly sensitive, possibly psychic and they have important life purposes.

  They have been incarnated on the planet to help to make a difference.

- **Deja vu** — A glimpse, photograph, movie image, feeling, sense, taste or smell of something that you have experienced before – perhaps in a previous life or just a sense of "knowing".

- **DMT (dimethyltry-ptamine)** — A psychedelic drug found in the plant and mammal kingdom.

  There is also evidence to support that the chemical is produced within the brain specifically by the pineal gland.

- **Gaia** — Is the personification of the Earth. The primal mother goddess of the Earth.

- **Holy Grail** — The Grail was said to be the cup of the Last Supper and used at the Crucifixion to receive blood flowing from Christ's side.

  However, it can also be seen symbolically as an image of the womb, creation and the divine feminine.

- **Incubus** — The male version of a Succubus.

- **Karma** — In Sanskrit means action, word or deed.

  It also refers to a spiritual principle of cause and effect whereby a person's actions can influence the future of that person.

- **Kundalini**　　In Sanskrit literally 'snake' an energy that lies at the base of the spine that when activated stimulates the sexual centres.

  If channelled up the spine can trigger creativity, rejuvenation and spiritual energies.

- **Monad**　　A monad is the higher self, soul aspect of a human being. An all-knowing, eternal and free from judgement centre of our being.

- **Om**　　The sound of "om" is a mantra – a vibration that is traditionally voiced at the beginning of Hindu and yoga sessions, and is a mantra that can be recited by anyone.

  It is meant to be the sound of creation – the universe was created through sound.

  The universe is a living, sentient being and as such vibrates at its own frequency. This frequency has been measured to be at 432 Hz and this is where the origin of Om or AUM originates from.

  This frequency is also found throughout nature and so the chanting of this sound brings one into harmony with the natural frequency of the universe and nature.

It is documented that chanting this sound affects the physical body, alters the nervous system and calms the mind/body as a result.

We usually hear this chant before and after meditation/yoga groups as a method to align people with cosmic unity.

- **Over shadowing**

Is when a medium is overtaken by a spirit. However there are more subtle instances of overshadowing, e.g. when a discarnate being comes close to an incarnated being to offer guidance or support.

- **Portal**

A dimensional doorway to travel.

- **Star / seed children**

Beings that have been incarnated on other planets and planetary systems. They come here on the earth plane in order to live as a human being, but knowing that they are from another planetary system.

These beings also display certain traits that are very similar to the crystal / indigo / rainbow child. In most cases they are highly evolved in spirituality.

- **Succubus**

Believed to be a feminine demon that seduces men.

- **The Rainbow Bridge** Mythical walkway into the realms of the spirit world.

  It is theorised by some that our loved ones wait on their side of the bridge to meet us when we pass.

  It also depicts a passage from one world to another.

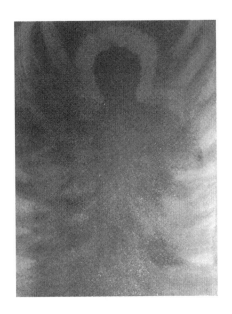

To be given love in all forms is to be very blessed.

To give love unconditionally opens your being...

In more ways than you can imagine...

*Just giving a stranger a smile can make a
difference to that person's day.*

*Above all, remember we get out of life what we
put in...*

Enjoy every minute, and most of all - be happy!!

About:

Annette Moss

Annette writes:

"I've always known I was different even as a small child. Being Sensitive is a great gift.

"Whilst growing up I was used to seeing and conversing with spirit, although I mainly saw spirits at night. They used to wake me up to talk to them. It wasn't until I reached adulthood that I have embraced my gift of communicating.

"I have been experiencing the wonderful world of spirit for many years. I am what you would call a Clairvoyant, Clairsentiant and Clairaudiant. This means that I can see spirit in a normal physical form and hear them via my own ears, or by thoughts placed within my head. I can also feel spirit which is fabulous as I can experience such emotions i.e. love.

"It is a great honour to feel the love that was once and is still shared.

"All of these gifts 'as I call them' help me to convey messages to loved ones. These are from spirits of people who have properly "passed over." I also see other souls who are semi-transparent, These souls may have been troubled, had unfinished business, or who were simply lost and needed passing over into the light.

"I now work very closely with the Spirit World and my aim is to prove that life in fact is eternal.

"I teach spiritual development classes and am available for workshops nationally, with programmes tailored to suit the class's needs. My demonstration of mediumship is offered to audiences from 20 to 200+. I also offer private 1:1 readings.

"I have worked alongside investigation companies (more commonly known as ghost hunters): it is amazing what information spirit people wish to share. I really do feel privileged."

Annette paints as a Spiritual Artist (including the paintings within this book and its front cover), and also offers a range of healing holistic therapies. She is a qualified Hypnotherapist and Spiritual Healer / Reiki Master.

Annette is also a Celebrant for Naming Ceremonies, Weddings, Hand Fastings, Vow Renewals, Funerals and End of Life. She can provide:

- The services of a Celebrant both before and during the ceremony

- Creation of a unique ceremony script (a full tailor-made script for a Bespoke Ceremony)

- Exclusive ceremony and event planning guides if choosing a Bespoke Ceremony

- The expertise of the Celebrant who will guide and advise you

- A certificate, signed during the ceremony.

Annette met Mark in 2008 when he came to her as a client for hypnotherapy, looking at his past lives.

Annette's Love and Light website can be found at: **www.annettesloveandlight.co.uk**.

Facebook pages:

www.facebook.com/annettesloveandlight and **www.facebook.com/AnnetteMossMedium**

Annette can be contacted by email: **annettemossmedium@gmail.com**

She invites you to share with her your spiritual experiences or to ask any questions you may have after reading this book. She may not be able to contact you back directly, but your messages may feed into future books.

Mark Firth

Mark from an early age has always intuitively felt there was more to life than our physical existence proved otherwise and his journey of spiritual self-discovery began during his early teenage years.

His research of the paranormal, UFO's, unexplained phenomena and spirituality led him to him begin his psychic development around 2001.

Since then Mark has continued studying spirituality, developing his clairaudience/clairsentience skills and has completed training in energy healing, sound therapy and Reiki.

He offers sound baths in his local area and can provide energy readings to the public when requested.

In his day to day work Mark works in special needs education teaching young people with autism and communication difficulties.

A job he has been doing since 2002 and one in which he is keen to bring his love of spirituality and its benefits to the classroom.

He offers his student's relaxation, meditation and sound healing as methods to cope with our increasingly stressful lives, and would like to expand his practice to offer sound therapy to more individuals with learning difficulties and autism.

If you would like to get in touch with Mark please contact him on sonicblessings@hotmail.co.uk

Angela Garry – Assistant and Series Editor

Angela Garry is a self-employed trainer for Personal Assistants and Administrative staff, and the author of two books for administrative professionals, plus 15 further books for adults and children. She is also the Editor of more than 15 books for other authors, and runs "EDPA", the leading magazine for PAs and Admins in education.

Angela first met Annette Moss in 2008 at a Personal Assistants' Networking event which was an evening of clairvoyance and a ghost walk in and around the grounds of the Breadsall Priory in Derby.

During the writing of this series, Angela has been involved in taking notes and dictation, scribing, creating the book layout, and editing the final volumes.

You can contact Angela via angelagarry@picaaurum.com